D1449731

The Stem Cell Debate

Titles in the Issues in Focus Today *series:*

Addictions and Risky Behaviors

Cutting, Bingeing, Snorting, and Other Dangers

ISBN 0-7660-2165-3

Am I Fat?

The Obesity Issue for Teens

ISBN 0-7660-2527-6

Attack of the Superbugs

The Crisis of Drug-Resistant Diseases

ISBN 0-7660-2400-8

Bullying

How to Deal With Taunting, Teasing, and Tormenting

ISBN 0-7660-2355-9

Dating, Relationships, and Sexuality

What Teens Should Know

ISBN 0-7660-1948-9

Downloading Copyrighted Stuff From the Internet

Stealing or Fair Use?

ISBN 0-7660-2164-5

High-Tech Babies

The Debate Over Assisted Reproductive Technology

ISBN 0-7660-2528-4

Other People's Words

What Plagiarism Is and How to Avoid It

ISBN 0-7660-2525-X

Peanut Butter, Milk, and Other Deadly Threats

What You Should Know About Food Allergies

ISBN 0-7660-2529-2

Resolving Conflicts

How to Get Along When You Don't Get Along

ISBN 0-7660-2359-1

You Have the Right to Know Your Rights

What Teens Should Know

ISBN 0-7660-2358-3

The Stem Cell Debate

The Ethics and Science
Behind the Research

ISSUES IN FOCUS TODAY

Laura Black

Enslow Publishers, Inc.
40 Industrial Road
Box 398
Berkeley Heights, NJ 07922
USA
http://www.enslow.com

To Todd—for your encouragement, support, and love

Library of Congress Cataloging-in-Publication Data

Black, Laura
    The stem cell debate : the ethics and science behind the research / Laura Black.
        p. cm. — (Issues in focus today)
    Includes bibliographical references and index.
    ISBN 0-7660-2545-4
    1. Stem cells—Research—Moral and ethical aspects—United States—Juvenile
literature. 2. Embryonic stem cells—Research—Moral and ethical aspects—United
States—Juvenile literature. 3. Human embryo—Research—Moral and ethical
aspects—United States—Juvenile literature. I. Title. II. Series.
QH588.S83B53 2006
174'.28—dc22

                                            2005037880

Printed in the United States of America

10 9 8 7 6 5 4 3 2 1

To Our Readers:
We have done our best to make sure that all Internet Addresses in this book were active
and appropriate when we went to press. However, the author and publisher have no control over and assume no liability for the material available on those Internet sites or on
other Web sites they may link to. Any comments or suggestions can be sent by e-mail to
comments@enslow.com or to the address on the back cover.

Illustration Credits: Photo by Richard Anderson, © University of Minnesota, pp. 37, 103;
AP/Wide World, pp. 5, 21, 86; Scott Bauer, U.S. Department of Agriculture/Agricultural
Research Service, pp. 71, 113; Corel Corp., pp. 74, 115; Dr. Edwin P. Ewing, Jr./Centers
for Disease Control, pp. 5, 81; © President and Fellows of Harvard University, pp. 15, 54;
Jeff LeClere, Iowa Herpetology, pp. 67, 111; Jeff Miller/University of Wisconsin-Madison,
pp. 3, 40, 78, 117; Photo Researchers, pp. 5, 98; Photos.com, p. 89; Christopher Reeve
Foundation, p. 11; Reeve-Irvine Research Center, pp. 51, 107; Roslin Institute, pp. 5, 59,
63, 109; Texas Heart Institute, pp. 5, 31; University of Pittsburgh, pp. 5, 24, 27, 101;
University of Wisconsin-Madison, pp. 5, 7, 47, 105; U.S. Department of Defense, p. 93.

Cover Illustrations: Su-Chun Zhang/University of Wisconsin-Madison (background);
Andrew Paul Leonard/Photo Researchers, Inc. (large inset photo); BananaStock (small
inset photo). Inset shows a color-enhanced scanning electron micrograph of a stem cell
collected from human bone marrow; background shows a cluster of neural cells derived
from human embryonic stem cells.

C o n t e n t s

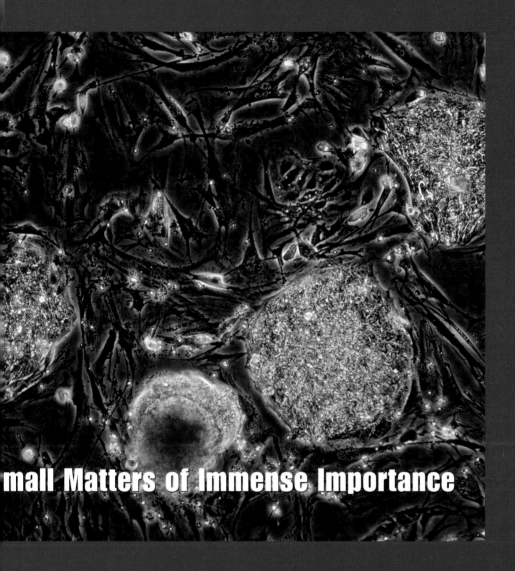

mall Matters of Immense Importance

Christopher Reeve rode his horse, Buck, out of the starting box at 3:01 P.M. on a sunny Memorial Day weekend in 1995. Having trained and raced horses for nearly a decade, he felt well prepared to lead his chestnut gelding over the eighteen jumps in this cross-country race through the rolling Virginia countryside.

The forty-two-year-old athletic and handsome actor, whose most famous role was that of the comic book hero Superman, knew what it meant to take risks. He did not put himself into dangerous situations unless he had first stacked the odds in his favor. As a result, his life was full of successful adventures. Reeve had flown an airplane solo across the Atlantic Ocean twice. He'd soared in a sailplane over Pikes Peak. He knew preparation was essential for any challenge in life. And he knew, that sunny afternoon, that he and Buck were ready for the challenging course ahead.

Nothing, however, could have prepared Reeve for what he faced minutes later, when Buck stopped short at the third fence, sending him head-first over the third jump, his hands entangled in the bridle. Reeve landed squarely on his head, fracturing two vertebrae in his neck. He was paralyzed from the neck down. There was no surgery, no medication, that could heal his damaged spine.

When he first realized what had happened, Reeve thought he would rather die. Very soon, though, as he wrote in his 1998 book, *Still Me*, he decided he had reason to live. He had his devoted wife, Dana, who after the accident had whispered in his ear, "You're still you. And I love you."[1] And he had a cause that he was uniquely qualified to further because of his fame as Superman—hope, for himself and others, that a cure for spinal cord injury might someday be found.

Reeve not only survived, he took on what some consider to be the greatest role of his life. For the next ten years, in addition to balancing his roles as husband, father, and a professional actor and director, he worked tirelessly to advocate better care for spinal cord injury patients. He founded the Christopher Reeve Foundation and raised millions of dollars for research into spinal cord injury repair. He also put a face on an effort to promote a highly controversial new type of research that is limited by federal funding—human embryonic stem cell research.

Christopher Reeve died on October 10, 2004. He never realized his dream to walk again, but one of the causes he came to champion—support for stem cell research—was vaulted into national attention. It became a key issue in the 2004 presidential election. It remains a hotly debated issue today.

Proponents of stem cell research say that an aggressively funded stem cell research program may someday usher in a new era in medicine. They think it will provide a world in which those who have suffered from spinal cord injury and those afflicted with other debilitating illnesses, such as Parkinson's and Alzheimer's disease, may be healed by a simple injection of made-to-order stem cells that could multiply and replace dead or diseased nerve cells; a world in which people with damaged or worn bone or cartilage could be healed by an injection of bone- or cartilage-producing stem cells. And, most tantalizing of all, a world in which patients in need of a kidney, heart, or lung transplant could turn to a medical specialist for tailor-made replacement organs.

"How'd you like to have your own personal biological repair kit standing by at the hospital?" Ronald Prescott Reagan, the son of former President Ronald Reagan, who died from Alzheimer's Disease in June 2004, asked in a speech to the Democratic National Convention in Boston shortly after his father's death. "Sound like magic?" Reagan asked. "Welcome to the future of medicine."[2]

For many Americans who share in Reeve's and Reagan's views on stem cell research, this future is one that medical researchers should—and must—pursue. Research intended to alleviate horrific human pain and suffering is more than a nice idea. It is, they contend, a moral obligation.

But for many others who have a different idea about what is just, this picture of the future of medical care is simply not worth the price.

Embryonic stem cell research, they say, will lead the United States down a "slippery slope." This means that once a society allows certain questionable actions to take place, those actions will eventually become commonplace. That, in turn, will lead to even more questionable actions to be proposed and permitted. Eventually, so the theory goes, society will have taken so many steps in the wrong direction that it would be difficult, if not impossible, to take a step back. Also, they say that human embryonic research should not be funded by the tax dollars of many Americans who recoil at such activity.

"We should not succumb to this latest campaign, but reflect on the ethical errors that brought us this far," Richard M. Doerflinger, Deputy Director of the Secretariat for Pro-Life Activities of the United States Conference of Catholic Bishops, told a congressional subcommittee in September 2004. "Because scientists, and the for-profit companies that increasingly support and make use of their research, are always tempted to treat helpless members of the human family as mere means to their ends, the rest of society—including government—must supply the urgently needed barrier against unethical exploitation of human beings."[3]

Those for, and those against, embryonic stem cell research have made very convincing arguments to support their claims. But what exactly are embryonic stem cells? Where do they come from? What is the difference between adult stem cells and embryonic stem cells? And what is this new type of stem cell research that Ron Reagan spoke of, which he and others say creates a simple mass of cells, not human embryos, from which human embryonic stem cells can be derived?

Stem Cells: The Definition

Stem cells are the human body's basic building blocks. They are responsible for the miraculous transformation of a fertilized egg into a child. In adults, they are responsible for the creation of new cells to replace worn-out or damaged cells. They create the new skin that heals a cut, for example, and the constant supply of new white blood cells, which fight off infectious organisms that enter the body. In one single human being alone, stem cells produce billions of new blood cells every day.

Christopher Reeve, who was paralyzed in a riding accident, supported human embryonic stem cell research aimed at treating spinal cord injury.

The National Institutes of Health (NIH) defines stem cells as having two important characteristics that distinguish them from all other cells of living organisms. First, stem cells are unspecialized cells that can renew themselves for long periods of time through cell division. In other words, they can re-create themselves many times over. Second, and most fascinating, is that under certain conditions, these cells can become specialized cells that have specific functions. They can become the beating cells of the heart muscle, blood cells, liver cells, or even brain cells.

Exactly how stem cells accomplish this is of great interest to medical researchers for many reasons. Stem cells can provide a window on the little understood genetic and molecular processes through which cells become specialized and organized into tissues and organs. This knowledge may be put to good use in solving what goes wrong when a cell does not develop properly, resulting, for example, in birth defects and disease. Stem cell research may also someday provide a source for transplantable cells and tissue, though all experts agree it will be years before these types of medical treatments are available. As with any scientific research, though, there are certainly no guarantees.

At present there are two main ways to go about stem cell research with either animal or human cells. Either scientists use adult stem cells or they use embryonic stem cells. (A few labs use human embryonic germ cells. These cells, which are similar in function to embryonic stem cells, are taken from the tissue of dead fetuses.[4])

Some scientists have suggested alternative ways to obtain human embryonic stem cells. While many applaud these proposals, others are still concerned about ethical issues involved.

Adult Stem Cells

Adult stem cells are found in mature tissue of children and adults. Though they have not been found in all tissue in the human body, they have been found in the blood, bone marrow, brain, liver, in fat, and even in baby teeth. Strictly speaking, adult stem cells are not always "adult" cells at all. They are also found in the umbilical cord blood of newborn infants and in the placenta, so they are more appropriately called "non-embryonic" stem cells. (However, in this book, and in most references to them, they are known as "adult stem cells.")

It is widely believed that adult stem cells serve as backups to their neighboring cells, differentiating into specialized tissue as needed to maintain the tissue or organ in which they reside. Some think that adult stem cells are limited in what they can become.[5] New research, however, is challenging this long-held belief.[6] Experiments suggest that some adult stem cells that reside within bone marrow may be capable of producing a wide variety of other types of specialized cells.[7] Some think there may be a "universal" adult stem cell that is activated by a signal, such as an injury, to "home" in and make repairs to damaged tissues or organs. Others propose that any specialized cell can be induced to participate in an organism's recovery from injury through a special cell function that is not yet understood.[8]

Stem cells are unspecialized cells that can renew themselves for long periods through cell division. And under certain conditions, they can become specialized cells that have specific functions.

Adult stem cells have been used in medical therapy for the past thirty years. The therapy they appear in is commonly called a bone marrow transplant. When patients receive donated marrow to restore their body's immune system (which fights off infection and disease), they receive infusions of stem cells that reside in the marrow, which, researchers now know, generate red and white blood cells, and cartilage, bone, and muscle tissue.

The stem cells that create blood cells are the best known of adult stem cells because researchers have been studying bone marrow for a very long time. Some scientists think that these bone marrow stem cells may also help generate several other types of specialized cells in addition to just blood cells. Researchers have not been able to use these cells in stem cell research as much as they would like, though, because they cannot survive for long outside a living organism.[9] They are also very difficult to find because they are hard to distinguish from other components in blood, and they exist in very small quantities. (Only one in every ten thousand cells in the marrow is a blood stem cell.)

Recent experiments designed to investigate adult stem cells and how they affect animals with certain conditions have given many people reason to believe that bone marrow adult stem cells could someday be useful for many other types of human treatments.

"Electrifying" was the word one reporter used to describe the work of researchers who in April 2001 announced they had created new heart muscle cells in mice simply by injecting the mice with their own adult bone marrow stem cells. The researchers, Donald Orlic and colleagues at the NIH and the New York Medical College, injected the stem cells directly into the damaged areas of the animals' hearts and then examined the hearts nine days later.[10] What they saw surprised many in the medical community: New heart cells appeared at the area of injury. This seemed unbelievable. Up to this point, it was thought that heart muscle cells, once destroyed, could not regrow.

Since then, other scientists have repeated this procedure in their laboratories—and medical doctors in other countries are using it to treat critically ill human heart patients. Doctors involved in a study in Brazil report that not only had many patients improved, but some have resumed their normal lives.[11]

There are now several clinical studies under way at American universities and hospitals to evaluate this new procedure using

Stem cells are remarkable for their ability to self-renew and—under certain conditions—become differentiated to perform specific functions.

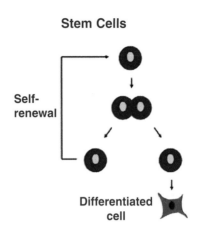

Stem Cells

Self-renewal

Differentiated cell

rigorous American standards. There are also studies testing the use of adult stem cells for other treatments, such as the repair of damaged knees. Many more researchers are probing adult stem cells under microscopes in hopes of gleaning knowledge about basic cell biology, or how cells develop and function, and how they interact with other cells within an organism.

One of the greatest challenges to using adult stem cells is based on the cells' level of development. Adult stem cells have already undergone changes; they are headed down a certain road toward becoming a specialized type of cell. Because of this, and because stem cells have not been found to exist in all parts of the human body, the kinds of therapies that might come from them may be somewhat limited. Another challenge is the fact that there is no convenient source of these cells. Researchers get human adult stem cells from samples of human body tissue, organs, and blood samples that contain many different types of cells. It is a challenge to isolate a stem cell from other cells as they look alike. Adult stem cells are also very hard to maintain in a lab and to amplify, or grow, into the large quantities needed for research purposes.[12]

A group of eighty Nobel Prize recipients wrote to President George W. Bush in February 2001, when the President was contemplating whether the federal government should fund human embryonic stem cell research. They said, "Some have suggested that adult stem cells may be sufficient to pursue all treatments for human disease. It is premature to conclude that adult stem cells have the same potential as embryonic stem cells. . . ."[13]

Embryonic Stem Cells

Embryonic stem cells are cells that occur at the earliest stages of human and animal development. They are virtually "blank slates" that can become any one of the 220 types of cells and tissue in the human body.[14]

Embryonic stem cells are derived from the inner cell mass of the four- or five-day-old developing egg cell, which at this stage is called a blastocyst. The thirty or so cells that have been taken from the inner cell mass of the blastocyst are transferred onto a plastic laboratory culture dish, where they grow and divide and, in time, crowd the dish. The cells are then gently removed and placed in separate, new culture dishes so that the original cells eventually yield millions of embryonic stem cells. The resulting collection of cells is called a stem cell line. It is important to note that the process of deriving the cells from the inner cell mass ends the embryo's development.

Most of the embryos from which embryonic stem cell lines are derived are created at clinics that perform in vitro fertilization (IVF) for people who cannot have a child through natural means. In these clinics, for each couple, about one dozen eggs are fertilized in a petri dish. Only a few are transferred into the woman's uterus. The remaining embryos are frozen for future use. When the embryos are no longer needed—for example, when a couple decides that their family is complete—the embryos are often discarded as medical waste.[15] Sometimes the embryos are donated to other couples through an embryo adoption program. Sometimes they are donated to science. As of April 4, 2002, there were approximately four hundred thousand embryos frozen in storage.[16]

While not one person has yet been cured using embryonic stem cells, experiments with rats and mice have produced interesting results:

- Rats with spinal injuries were able to walk—and some to run—after a researcher injected them with human embryonic stem cells that were coaxed to become a type of brain cell known as an oligodendrocyte.[17]

- When cells derived from human embryonic stem cells were transplanted into mice who had conditions similar to those of Type 1 diabetes, symptoms were reversed.[18] (Type 1 diabetes is a disorder in which the levels of glucose—a simple sugar that is the body's fuel—in the blood are unusually high because the body lacks insulin. Insulin is a hormone that helps transport glucose into every cell in the body.)

- Mice that were bred to have a faulty immune system regained function of that system after injections of their own cloned embryonic stem cells that were genetically "repaired" in a laboratory.[19]

While experiments have shown potential, there are several challenges that researchers must address before embryonic stem cells can be tried in treatments for human patients. To begin with, scientists must first figure out how to coax a cell to become a certain type of specialized cell. This is because experiments have shown that embryonic stem cells injected into animals can develop into tumors.

Alternative Sources for Embryonic Stem Cells

A few alternative sources for stem cells have been suggested in the past few years so that embryos are not needed and ethical issues are avoided. Most of these suggestions, though, have also been met with objection by people who think these alternatives are just destroyed human embryos made in a laboratory.

- *Nuclear transfer.* Some people think that nuclear transfer (NT) should be used to create laboratory-grown cell masses from which human embryonic stem cells could be obtained. Some stem cell researchers call NT "somatic cell nuclear transfer," or SCNT. (A somatic cell is any cell in the body other than the reproductive cells.) This approach, they say, would make it unnecessary to use "spare" embryos, and it would provide a way to create custom-made cells from a patient's very own DNA.

  Nuclear transfer works like this: A patient's DNA is transferred to an egg cell that has had its own genetic material removed. The egg is then stimulated to grow. After four or five days, stem cells are derived from the growing cellular mass.

- *Parthenotes.* Parthenotes are unfertilized human eggs in laboratory culture dishes that have been stimulated to grow through chemicals or electrical stimulation. Stem cells can be extracted from the growing cell masses after a certain amount of development. Scientists say parthenotes could never become babies, even when placed in a uterus.

- *Biological artifacts.* Some medical researchers are investigating whether stem cells for human use could be derived from "embryolike structures," which they call artifacts, that could be created in the laboratory by deleting or changing the genetic information that an embryo or stimulated egg needs to develop properly. However, much discussion needs to occur, and much work needs to be done, to determine what type of biological artifact would be acceptable to create. Society would have to decide, for example, what "minimum parts" would define that structure as a human embryo, rather than just a mass of cells.[20]

Stem Cell Research Regulations in the United States

In response to a rising chorus of objections to the use of human embryos in stem cell research—and to concerns about ways that embryonic stem cells might be obtained through laboratory techniques—President George W. Bush in 2001 decided to review national stem cell research policy. He sought to create a policy that would allow some human embryonic stem cell work but that would discourage further destruction of human embryos.[21]

The President's new guidelines, announced in August 2001, for the first time allowed federal dollars to fund embryonic stem cell research—but only under certain conditions. Scientists seeking federal funding for human embryonic stem cell research were told that they must limit their research to some sixty stem cell lines created before August 9, 2001. These stem cell lines were derived from embryos created for reproductive purposes in IVF clinics.

As Bush explained in a national address, the stem cell lines permitted for research arose from a situation "where the life and death decision has already been made" and the stem cell lines were already in use by the scientific community.

"Embryonic stem cell research offers both great promise and great peril," Bush said, noting that in exploring the issue he kept coming back to two fundamental questions: Are frozen embryos human life, and if frozen embryos are routinely destroyed in IVF clinics anyway, should not they be used "for a greater good"?

"Leading scientists tell me research on these 60 lines has great promise that could lead to breakthrough therapies and cures," Bush said. "This allows us to explore the promise and potential of stem cell research without crossing a fundamental moral line, by providing taxpayer funding that would sanction or encourage further destruction of human embryos that have at least the potential for life."[22]

Researchers and advocates of embryonic stem cell research contend the 2001 Bush administration regulations are hampering the field of research, as only twenty-two of those original lines are actually available for research, according to the International Society for Stem Cell Research. Scientists would like to have access to new stem cell lines created in private labs after August 9, 2001.

"Many opportunities are being missed," stated stem cell expert George Daley, of the Children's Hospital in Boston and Harvard Medical School. In an opinion piece in the August 12, 2004, *New England Journal of Medicine*, Daley said: "The science of human embryonic stem cells is in its infancy, and the current policies threaten to starve the field at a critical stage."[23]

Many new stem cell lines have been created in private labs since the President's announcement, Daley reported, lines that are far superior to those available to federal researchers because the old lines were grown in culture dishes lined with mouse cells. (The mouse cells provide nutrients that maintain the human embryonic stem cells in an undifferentiated state.) Research has shown that stem cells grown on mouse cells absorb certain chemical compounds from the animal cells—compounds that the human immune system would target and destroy if they were introduced into the human body.[24] Some new stem cell lines are grown on human feeder cells and some on concoctions that are completely free of any animal molecules.

The 2001 guidelines do not restrict researchers from seeking funding from sources other than the federal government. Many researchers have turned to private companies and some states that are now offering financial support in hopes that the investment might someday yield a big return, both in future medical treatments and in financial gain.

California has made the biggest investment yet. In the 2004 November election, Californians voted to invest $3 billion over the next ten years in the California Institute for Regenerative

Medicine. By comparison, the federal government in 2003 funded $24.8 million in embryonic stem cell research projects and $190.7 million in nonembryonic human stem cell research.[25]

California was not the first to make the investment. In early 2004, New Jersey legalized human embryonic stem cell research and established the Stem Cell Institute of New Jersey. In early 2005, New Jersey's governor, Richard Codey, announced a plan that he hoped would allow the state to invest $380 million in stem cell research.

Wisconsin's governor in late 2004 announced plans to invest $750 million over the next several years. Connecticut in 2005 passed legislation to create a fund to provide $10 million a year

Ron Reagan, son of former president Ronald Reagan, spoke at the 2004 Democratic National Convention in support of stem cell research.

over ten years for stem cell research. And in April 2006, Maryland's legislature approved of investing up to $15 million in stem cell research in 2007.

Many other states are now debating whether they should permit—or criminalize—this work within their boundaries and whether state money should fund it. Many countries are also discussing how to regulate stem cell research within their borders.

In 2001, Britain cleared the way for an aggressive embryonic stem cell research program by passing a law permitting the therapeutic cloning of human embryos for research.[26] In 2004, it granted its first license to clone human embryos for research purposes.[27] A second license was awarded in early 2005.[28]

The Controversy: Moral and Ethical Questions

As funding for embryonic stem cell research becomes more readily available from private sources and from some states, and as news of advances and scandals in stem cell research in other countries makes front-page headlines, the debate about how to proceed with embryonic stem cell research continues to gain momentum.

Most of the arguments against this research are based on the belief that advances in adult stem cell research make embryonic stem cell research unnecessary and, even more importantly, the belief that embryos should not be destroyed for any reason. Advances in stem cell research have forced many people to think about when life begins—and what a human life is.

Is a four-day-old fertilized egg—a blastocyst consisting of some 100 to 150 cells—a human life? For some, a human being is created when a new, unique human genome is created, either inside a woman's uterus or in a petri plate. (A genome is an organism's genetic "fingerprint," defined by its DNA. It is a blueprint that makes that organism unique from all others.) Some people think that such an entity is not really "human" unless it is the combination of human egg and sperm, developing inside a mother's body. Still others think a growing fertilized egg, even inside a uterus, is not a human life until it has successfully implanted in the uterus, or after it has developed for at least fourteen days—the point at which it is no longer possible for that cell mass to divide and produce twins or triplets.

Is an embryolike structure created through cloning techniques truly just a simple mass of cells—or is it a cloned human life?

Leaders and policy makers today cannot ignore the stem cell issue. As headlines announce news of scientific advances, proponents for and against stem cell research press harder to support their views. Should the United States allow and fund embryonic stem cell research? Should it allow nuclear transfer? Or should it only permit and fund adult stem cell research?

There is little objection to adult stem cell research—but there is objection by many scientists, patient advocacy groups, and others to limiting stem cell research to experiments using *only* adult stem cells. Many advances are being made with adult stem cells. So why are some scientists not content with using them—exclusively—in their studies?

Adult Stem Cell Research

2

There is little objection to the use of adult stem cells for research and for future medical therapies because adult stem cells are not derived from embryos. However, there is much disagreement as to whether stem cell research can get as far, as fast, using only adult stem cells.

For many people who object to the use of human embryos in research, adult stem cells are an obvious solution. They point to experiments that suggest that injections of adult stem cells can help repair damaged hearts and to research that hints that some adult stem cells are somewhat plastic (meaning that they can create many types of specialized cells other than the type of tissue in which they are found). One of the most asked questions in the debate over whether to conduct human embryonic stem cell research is why scientists are not satisfied with using only adult stem cells in their experiments. What type of work is being done with adult stem cells, and what, if any, are the limitations?

What Are Adult Stem Cells?

Adult stem cells are those found in blood, tissue, and organs of children and adults. They have also been found in the after-products of birth, including umbilical cord blood and placenta. What adult stem cells do naturally in the body seems to depend upon where they are found. For example, stem cells in the blood produce blood cells, and stem cells in the liver produce liver cells.

No one really knows the origin of these cells. One theory suggests that they are leftover fetal cells that have been restrained from specializing. Another suggests they may be cells that for some reason, such as nearby injury, have gone back to a more primitive state.

In order to qualify as a stem cell, a cell must be able to renew itself indefinitely, and it must also produce other cells that go on to create more specialized cells. It is thought the adult stem cell does this by splitting into two: One of these is an exact copy of the original cell, and the other is called a progenitor cell. Progenitor cells divide and give rise to specialized cells.[1] One of the biggest challenges that scientists face is that it is very difficult to tell adult stem cells and progenitor cells apart.[2] This is a difficult problem because any cell sample taken from a living body contains a mixture of many different types of cells. It is no small task to isolate one specific type of adult stem cell in pure form.[3]

The most well known and widely studied of all adult stem cells is the blood stem cell, known as the hematopoietic stem cell (HSC). These cells reside in the blood and the bone marrow. (Bone marrow is a dense, fatty substance in the cavity of bones that resembles thick blood.) HSCs have been used in research for the past fifty years and are now routinely used to treat patients with cancers and other disorders of the blood and immune system. This treatment is commonly known as a bone marrow transplant.

Other adult stem cells that also have been studied and known for many years are mesenchymal stem cells (MSCs), which, like HSCs, are found in the bone marrow. These cells generate muscle, cartilage, bone, fat, and connective tissue.

Adult stem cells have been identified in many other parts of the human body, including the liver, muscle, fat, and baby teeth. A very surprising discovery has been the identification of neural stem cells, or adult stems cells in the brain. Some researchers have reported identifying adult stem cells in the heart, but there are many in the scientific community who question this claim.

In 2002, scientists at the University of Minnesota reported isolating a cell from the bone marrow that seemed to have the same potential as a pluripotent stem cell. A pluripotent cell is one that can generate all types of cells except for those, like the placenta, that develop to nourish an embryo growing in a uterus. The researcher named this type of cell a multipotent adult progenitor cell. While many scientists are excited about this discovery, so far only a few researchers have been able to isolate and sustain it in a lab.[4]

Adult Stem Cells as Treatments

As mentioned earlier, adult stem cells from bone marrow have been used for the past fifty years to treat patients with blood and immune disorders and cancer. Medical experts are now investigating whether stem cells could be used to treat other human ailments. So far, studies using bone marrow to repair damaged hearts have advanced the furthest.

In August 2005, a doctor in Japan reported that a heart attack patient who had received an injection of adult stem cells had improved so dramatically that the artificial heart that had kept the patient alive had been disconnected, and the patient, in good health, discharged from the hospital.[5]

Medical researchers from around the world—including the patient's doctor—thought the recovery was nothing short of remarkable. They all asked the same question: Were the adult

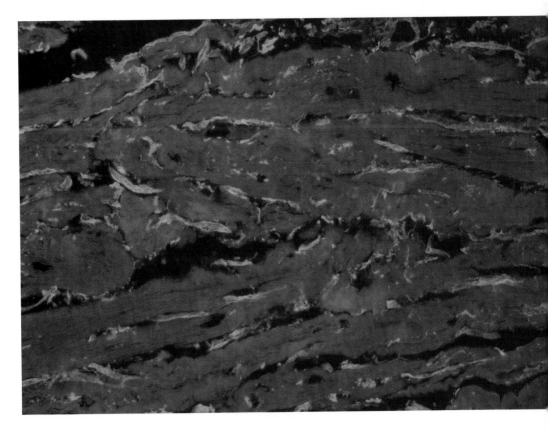

This is a close-up of adult stem cells taken at the University of Pittsburgh. In contrast to research with human embryonic stem cells, there is little opposition to research with adult stem cells.

stem cells, taken from the patient's own bone marrow and injected into her damaged heart, responsible for the recovery?

Not everyone agrees how effective such adult stem cell therapies really are for repairing the human heart. In fact, the subject is highly controversial. But success stories from other countries, and success in animal models in American laboratories, have prompted the U.S. Food and Drug Administration (FDA) to approve of several clinical trials to investigate whether these cells really can mend damaged hearts and, if so, how they do it. (The FDA is the national agency that regulates drugs and treatments for human use.) In May 2005, the University of Pittsburgh received FDA approval to inject a patient's own bone marrow stem cells into the heart during heart assist device surgery. In August 2005, it received permission to inject the cells during heart bypass surgery. Johns Hopkins School of Medicine received FDA approval to begin a study in March 2005 to inject MSCs into heart attack patients' bloodstreams.

> For many people who object to the use of human embryos in research, adult stem cells are an obvious solution.

One of the very first stem cell trials in the United States, organized by the Texas Heart Institute in 2004, is building on a study that was started in Brazil in 2001. In that study, fourteen patients received an average of fifteen injections containing about 2 million stem cells each. The cells were drawn from the patients' own bone marrow about four hours before the injections.[6] The doctors involved are convinced that injecting adult stem cells into patients' hearts heals those hearts. They tell stories, for example, of desperately ill patients who, several months after therapy, resumed normal lives. One patient returned to work. Others took up jogging.[7] "These people in Brazil were reborn. The stem cells 'woke up' their hearts," said Emerson

Perin, director of the new Interventional Cardiology/Stem Cell Institute at the Texas Heart Institute.[8] (Perin performed the stem cell injections into the Brazilian patients.)

In July 2005, Perin and the other doctors involved had an opportunity to inspect the heart of one of the patients. (The patient had died from unrelated causes.) They found an increase in the number of blood vessels in the area of the heart injected with stem cells.

"We believe this is the first time we have achieved clear documentation in a human heart that there is formation of new blood vessels at the site of stem cell injections—and we're very excited about that," said renowned cardiologist James Willerson, president of the institute and of the University of Texas Health Science Center.[9]

While medical experts are encouraged, some basic science researchers are reserved, and some are even skeptical. They cite statistics from ten different studies that suggest that adult stem cell injections only moderately improve heart function.[10]

It is possible that the improved heart function in the human patients may have been due to factors related to the treatment and not the treatment itself. The injections may have caused inflammation that then improved the hearts' blood flow, or the cells may have secreted hormones that stimulated the patients' existing heart cells to function better.[11] The basic science, said Irving Weissman, a leading adult stem cell researcher at Stanford University, is not very well understood, and until it is, these clinical trials might "in fact place a group of sick patients at risk."[12] One of the risks is the possibility that these injected adult stem cells may "misbehave" and form tumors.

Others expressed a different opinion: "The basic-science guys don't see patients that are going to die, but I have to look them in the face every day," Perin, of the Texas Heart Institute, told a *New York Times* reporter after the results were made public in 2005. "It's ludicrous to say we must understand the molecular mechanisms before we can try anything."[13]

A Long History of Clinical Use

In a way, adult stem cells have been used to treat patients with life-threatening diseases for the past one hundred years, although in the earliest attempts, doctors did not know there was such a thing as stem cells. These early treatments, for those with blood-related illnesses, were in the form of potions that patients had to drink. The potions included the ingredient human bone marrow, which medical experts today know contains adult stem cells.[14]

The first use of adult stem cells in modern medicine was the bone marrow transplant, which was first attempted in France in the 1950s to help people who were exposed to a radiation accident. The first successful transplant took place in the United States in 1968, when doctors from the University of Minnesota transferred the healthy bone marrow of a young girl to her four-month-old brother, who had an immune disorder. (This means his body could not fight off infections.) The boy's health was completely restored following the operation.[15]

Today, bone marrow transplants—which some scientists now refer to as "stem cell transfers"—are commonplace, especially for patients whose bodies have stopped producing the right amounts or kinds of blood cells, who have cancer, or whose bone marrow is destroyed by chemotherapy undertaken to destroy cancer cells. Doctors do not extract bone marrow to obtain stem cells: They get them from blood drawn from a donor instead. In this new procedure, the donor receives injections of a drug that draws the HSCs out of the marrow so that more of the HSCs are present in the donor's blood. This procedure is much easier on the donor than the previous method, which involved inserting a long needle into the hip bone to extract the marrow.[16]

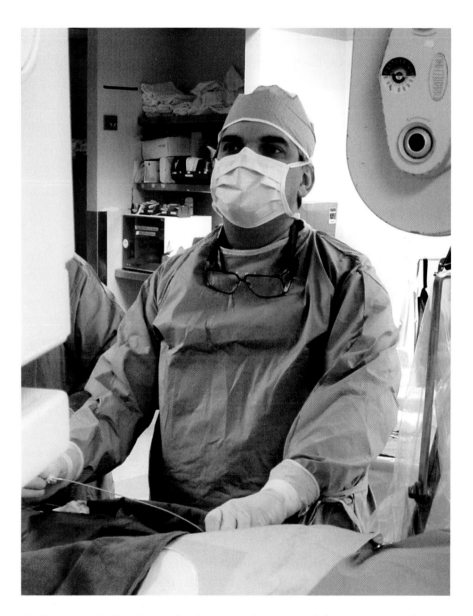

Dr. Emerson Perin, shown in the operating room, injected stem cells into patients' hearts. The patients' health improved, and it was found that the number of blood vessels in the injected hearts had increased.

Stem cell transfer is common due in large part to an advanced understanding of how the human immune system works. Scientists now know that in order for a transplant to be accepted by a patient's body, the donated material must be histocompatible. This means that it must carry the same antigens, or proteins, on the surface of its cells as the patient's normal body cells. If the antigens are different, the patient's immune system will create antibodies and other substances to destroy the donated cells.

The National Marrow Donor Program (NMDP), the non-profit organization that maintains a national registry of donors, coordinates an average of two hundred blood cell transfers in the United States each month for patients who do not have matching donors in their families. It has coordinated more than twenty thousand since the organization was founded in 1986.[17] (More than 5.5 million potential donors are registered with the NMDP. The organization also keeps records on forty thousand units of umbilical cord blood.)

Hematopoietic Stem Cells

HSCs—the stem cells that are so effective in these treatments—generate all of an organism's blood products. This includes red blood cells, which carry oxygen; white blood cells, which fight off infections; and platelets, which are necessary for blood to clot. They are sometimes called the "premier" adult stem cells because of their amazing ability to self-renew in an organism. What is more, experiments have shown that one single HSC can rebuild the entire blood system of a sick mouse.[18] This ability—the rescue of an entire blood system—has become a standard method scientists use to prove that isolated cells are really HSCs.

There is a growing body of evidence that HSCs may be able to participate in the generation of other types of cells in the body.[19] Some scientists have reported that HSCs, in laboratory dishes, can create cells that look like the three major types of brain cells, skeletal muscle cells, cardiac muscle cells, and liver cells.[20] These claims, though, are "the subject of intense scientific controversy."[21]

Many people are investing in the power of HSCs by banking the umbilical cord blood of their newborn children, which contains a small supply of HSCs. The blood can be frozen for about ten years. The U.S. House of Representatives in May 2005 voted to create a national cord blood program to preserve cord blood in public "banks" for general use. The program is overseen by the NMDP, which has been expanded to serve as the new national clearinghouse for umbilical cord blood as well as for bone marrow. It has also been given a new title: the C.W. Bill Young Cell Transplantation Program.

As with any transplant, an umbilical blood donation must be histocompatible with the patient or the donation will be destroyed in the patient's body. Some scientists think this problem of matching patients to donations may become a thing of the past, though, as new research has shown that a donation that is highly purified—meaning that it contains a very high concentration of HSCs and few of the other things found in blood—is far less likely to be rejected by a patient's body. Cord blood will likely prove to be useful in the future as more scientists investigate its potential.[22]

Many researchers are now working to find ways that HSCs can be used more widely in therapies, such as in the heart repair studies, but there are technical challenges that must be overcome before HSCs can be studied more widely in research. One of the biggest challenges to date is that HSCs do not easily self-renew outside of the living organism.[23] This makes them difficult to study in a laboratory. They are also difficult to distinguish from other blood cells in the bone marrow and bloodstream, which makes it challenging to obtain a pure sample of HSCs.[24] HSCs are also rare: Only one in every ten thousand cells in bone marrow, and one in every one hundred thousand cells circulating in the blood, is an HSC.[25]

Mesenchymal Stem Cells

Many people believe that MSCs hold the greatest promise for future clinical treatments. Like HSCs, they can generate many different types of cells. In laboratory experiments, MSCs have been coaxed to express genes—or to look and behave—like cells from many different parts of the body. In experiments using live animals, they appear to contribute to numerous types of tissues. But unlike HSCs, they can be obtained in sufficient quantities, which is necessary if they are ever to be used for human treatments, and, what is more, they can be maintained in a laboratory setting.[26] As a result, scientists are enthusiastic about the potential of MSCs for future medical studies.[27]

Several different research experiments using animals suggest that introducing HSCs and MSCs into certain types of damaged tissue may help to restore tissue function.

Johns Hopkins researchers made international headlines in November 2004 when they reported that they were able to repair the damaged hearts of pigs that had suffered heart attacks simply by injecting MSCs directly into the pigs' damaged heart muscle. Of fourteen pigs enrolled in the study, the seven who received the treatment had a nearly full recovery. The seven that did not died within two months.

In a commissioned paper written for the President's Council on Bioethics in 2004, David Prentice summarized some experiments in which adult stem cells were injected into mice. Prentice is a senior fellow at the Family Research Council, a Christian organization that opposes embryonic stem cell research. He is a former professor at Indiana State University and adjunct professor at the Indiana University School of Medicine. (Bioethics is the study of the impact on society of decisions in the areas of biology, medicine, and the environment.) Prentice mentioned several findings in his summary:

- When bone marrow stem cells were injected into the eyes of mice, the cells incorporated into the eye blood network.[28]

- Studies following genetically marked bone marrow stem cells in mice and rats suggested that the cells could "participate" in restoring damaged kidney tissue.[29]

- Bone marrow stem cells introduced into mice formed functioning liver cells and helped restore the animals' liver function.[30]

Prentice also noted that adult stem cells, when injected into animals, are somehow able to "home" to damaged tissue.[31]

Texas researchers in 2004 decided to put this suspected homing ability to the test and to good use. They manipulated the DNA of MSCs so that it included instructions to trigger the body to produce an anticancer treatment. They then injected those cells into mice with breast cancer. The stem cells acted like "guided missiles," targeting the cancerous cells and producing high concentrations of the anticancer treatment.[32]

This homing ability is an unexplained phenomenon, and some think it opens up a new way of thinking about how adult stem cells could be used for treatments.

"Rather than hunting for a patient's stem cells to remove, cultivate and then replace them, we may be able to summon the body's hidden stores," Robert Lanza and Nadia Rosenthal, leading stem cell researchers, reported in *Scientific American* in June 2004.[33] Rosenthal reported that MSCs in her stem cell experiments traveled great distances to reach an injury that was "tagged" with a certain protein.

Some scientists caution that these experiments were done with mice, and that results may differ in humans.

"We need to understand much more about the differences between mouse and human stem cells if we are to harness their potential," the National Academy of Sciences concluded in its 2002 report *Stem Cells and the Future of Regenerative Medicine.*[34]

Multipotent Adult Progenitor Cells

The existence of an adult stem cell that can generate nearly any type of specialized cell would be a big breakthrough for adult stem cell science. Many doubt that there is such a thing, but the work of one researcher at the University of Minnesota, however, has given many people reason to think twice.

In 2002, a research team led by Catherine Verfaillie, director of the University of Minnesota Stem Cell Institute, reported isolating a type of adult stem cell from human bone marrow that appeared to be able to specialize into many different types of cells. They called the cell a multipotent adult progenitor cell (MAPC). Beginning with MSCs, which in an organism generate bone, cartilage, and fat, Verfaillie and her colleagues worked tirelessly to produce a highly pure concentration of what appeared to be a different type of stem cell. Experiments showed the cells were capable of generating other cells that appeared, in laboratory analysis, to be very much like other types of cells, including those found in the brain and liver.[35] When injected into mouse embryos, the cells were found in many of the animals' tissues, suggesting that they had developed into that type of tissue.[36]

Only a handful of labs have been able to repeat Verfaillie's results. Even in her own lab, Verfaillie said, the method to isolate MAPCs works less than half the time. Among those who have tried to repeat her work is Irving Weissman, a professor at Stanford University and director of the Stem Cell Institute at Stanford University School of Medicine. Weissman, the first to isolate blood cells in mice and in humans, said he thinks the research is very important and may lead to new medical cures.

Catherine Verfaillie, director of the University of Minnesota Stem Cell Institute, led a team that isolated the multipotent adult progenitor cell.

However, the failure of other labs to repeat the results raises serious questions about the existence of such a truly pluripotent adult stem cell.[37]

The Challenges

According to the NIH, adult stem cells have "enormous potential" for basic science research and for development of future therapies.[38] There are challenges to overcome, though, before the research is translated into effective and safe treatments.

One challenge is that even though they have been found in many different places throughout the human body, adult stem cells have not been found in every single tissue and organ.

Where they are known to exist, they are found in small numbers, which makes isolating them from samples a challenge. Also, the number of stem cells inside a living organism appears to decrease with age, and those that are found may have had genetic damage owing to the simple fact that they have existed, inside an adult's body, for a long time.

More problematic is the fact that scientists do not yet know to what extent adult stem cells are truly able to specialize into a different type of cell. "New" specialized cells created by adult stem cells may look like a certain type of cell, based on the detection of certain chemicals, but no one knows if they would actually function like that cell inside a human body.[39] (The same question can be asked of embryonic stem cells that differentiate into specialized cells in a laboratory dish.) One theory speculates that adult stem cells are simply fusing with neighboring, mature adult cells.[40] Another proposes that they simply summon other cells to the site of repair.[41]

Some scientists speak of an "uncertainty principle" about the behavior of adult stem cells—actually, about the behavior of any type of cell used in laboratory experiments. The idea goes something like this: Isolating an adult stem cell from its environment, and then putting that cell through various laboratory tests, alters the stem cell's environment. If a cell takes its cues from its surrounding environment, is the cell itself altered in this process?[42] As one scientist stated: "The cells in our hands and in our laboratories are not the same as they were in the body."[43]

Slow but Steady Research

People who believe that adult stem cells could be used exclusively think that in time, with continued slow but steady research, adult stem cells will provide safe, effective therapies that do not involve ethical problems. Improved laboratory techniques, they hope, may help overcome many of the present challenges. Also, if a truly pluripotent adult stem cell is found in the human body, or if HSCs and MSCs can be used somehow to summon help from other cells, it may be unnecessary to find adult stem cells in every human tissue and organ.

Adult stem cell research makes sense, they say, because an adult stem cell taken from a patient's body would not be rejected by that patient's immune system when it is reintroduced for therapy. In other words, a patient's very own cells could be used to treat a condition or disease—so long as the stem cells themselves are disease-free.

There is one technical issue, though, that stands in the way of progress. Even if adult stem cell researchers do discover an adult stem cell that can become any cell in the body, scientists must figure out how to coax that stem cell to generate specific types of cells. This is a hurdle for both adult and embryonic stem cell researchers, because without this knowledge, stem cells of any type cannot safely be used for treatments. Truly pluripotent stem cells may spontaneously form tumors.

At the moment—for both adult and embryonic stem cell researchers—the triggers that direct stem cells to differentiate and become specialized cells, are, overall, a mystery.

Human Embryonic Stem Cell Research

When President George W. Bush in early 2001 was wrestling with how human embryonic stem cell research should be regulated, a renowned brain surgeon offered a simple image to put the stem cell situation in America in perspective.

"The genie," said Stan Pelofsky, president of the American Association of Neurological Surgeons, was "out of the bottle."[1]

The genie, of course, was embryonic stem cell research, which was already being conducted in private laboratories across the nation. It was also under way in many more labs across the globe, in countries whose regulations were far less restrictive. Whether it really would someday lead to a new era in the medical sciences, providing previously impossible cures, remained to be seen. Whether it was cruel hype, as many claimed it to be, or hope, as enthusiastic researchers suggested, was unknown. One thing was obviously clear: It and the controversy about it were unlikely to vanish any time soon.

Many scientists want to use embryonic stem cells in their work for numerous reasons. To begin with, the cells can be derived from the four-day-old blastocyst with relative ease: They are not hidden in a mixture of cells taken from a blood or tissue sample of a living organism. Most of all, they are capable of becoming any cell in the body, and they can proliferate for a very long time in a lab.

But what exactly is a blastocyst? And what do scientists mean by "derived"?

Those who support human embryonic stem cell research, and those who are against it, use highly technical terms to present their side of the issue. These scientific terms are not words heard in everyday conversation. They are terms, though, that have become a critical part of the debate because so much of the controversy about human embryonic stem cell research is based on opinion as to when human life begins.

A background in embryology, the study of the development of the human embryo, is useful for understanding these terms and the reasons why there is such disagreement.

Human Embryology

Scientists differ on the exact definition of the word "embryo." Most agree, though, that in humans this word refers to a fertilized egg cell during the first two months of its development. After two months, the embryo is called a fetus.

In the normal series of events leading to the birth of a human being, a human egg cell is fertilized by a sperm cell shortly after the egg is released by the ovary. Fertilization usually takes place in the fallopian tube, while the egg is on its way to the uterus. Immediately after fertilization, the genetic material of the egg cell combines with that of the sperm cell to create a new, unique genome, or genetic blueprint. At this point, the fertilized egg is called a zygote. The zygote begins dividing, eventually growing into a solid mass of cells that completes the journey to the uterus about six days after fertilization.

Scientists often use the term "totipotent" to describe the cells of the zygote at this point in its development. A totipotent cell is one that can become any cell known to exist in an organism, including becoming an entire organism by itself.

By the time the embryo enters the uterine cavity, it resembles a hollow, fluid-filled ball. At this point in its development, it is called a blastocyst, a term derived from the Greek word for "bud" or "germ."

The outer cells of the blastocyst are known as the trophoblast. These are the cells that enable the blastocyst to implant, or attach to the uterus. The trophoblast also eventually helps to form the placenta, the organ that nourishes the fetus.

A cluster of cells growing along the inside wall of the blastocyst is called the inner cell mass. These cells will form the fetus. These are the cells that scientists isolate, and out of which grow the embryonic stem cells.

The stem cells from this inner cell mass are considered to be pluripotent. This means they can generate almost all cells of the body—but not all. These cells, for example, could not create trophoblast cells. Only a totipotent cell, such as the early zygote, is capable of such work.

It is important to note that most of the blastocysts, or embryos, from which stem cells are derived for research are created at IVF clinics. These private, for-profit clinics serve people who are unable to conceive children through natural means. In IVF, egg and sperm are united in laboratory culture dishes. In most instances, about a dozen zygotes, or embryos, are created for every couple, but only a few are transferred to a mother's uterus in the hope that it will continue to develop and a child eventually will be born. The remaining embryos are frozen and stored so that the couple can attempt to initiate another pregnancy at a later date. Often, when a family is complete and the embryos are no longer needed, they are destroyed, donated to other couples, or donated for scientific research. Blastocysts that research scientists obtain to create human embryonic stem cell lines are unused embryos that are created in IVF laboratories and donated to research by the clinic with the clients' understanding and permission.

Understanding what happens next to a human embryo that is developing normally inside a human uterus following the fifth day of fertilization is very useful in understanding the finer points of the arguments for and against human embryonic stem cell research. This is because of certain milestones in the development of the blastocyst after implantation.

In the natural setting, if all goes well, the blastocyst enters the uterus at day six or seven and begins to implant in the uterine wall. After the twelfth day, the embryo is fully implanted. The inner cell mass begins to form layers, and sometime during the third week, a thick band of cells called the primitive streak begins to develop. The primitive streak is often referred to during policy discussions and debates because one end of the streak begins to form the head end of the embryo, and it is here that the beginning of the nervous system appears.[2]

Also during the third week, three germ layers appear in the streak. The word "germ" refers to "the beginning." These are the layers of cells that generate the three different categories of cells in a living organism. The mesoderm gives rise to muscle, skeleton, connective tissue, and blood vessels; the ectoderm gives rise to the skin, the nervous system, and the eyes, ears, and nose; and the endoderm produces the linings of the digestive and respiratory systems.

Another important milestone in development that is often referred to in the stem cell research controversy is the fourteenth day of development. Up until the fourteenth day, it is possible for the growing cell mass to split into two or more parts, creating multiple births. It is rare for an embryo to "cleave," as it is called, and produce twins or other multiple individuals, after the fourteenth day.

The First Human Embryonic Stem Cells in the Lab

The first research team to successfully isolate and then maintain human embryonic stem cells in a laboratory setting was led by James Thomson, a University of Wisconsin professor. Thomson published the results of his work in the November 1998 issue of *Science*, a well-known and highly respected scientific journal. The achievement ended a seventeen-year international "race" to be first to culture human stem cells after mouse embryonic stem cells were successfully isolated in 1981.[3]

Almost simultaneously, a second American researcher, John Gearhart, of Johns Hopkins University, reported that his research team had cultured similar cells, though the stem cells they extracted were not from a blastocyst, but from nonliving fetal tissue.[4] These cells are called human embryonic germ cells, or HEGCs for short.

Both scientists had developed a method to culture, or grow, the stem cells in abundance in the lab by providing a suitable culture, or environment, for the cells to live in. The cells simply did what stem cells naturally do—they multiplied through simple cell division, with each cell creating two exact copies of itself.

Today scientists do not have to obtain embryos in order to acquire embryonic stem cells. The cells are available for research purposes from other laboratories that specialize in creating human embryonic stem cell lines. A qualifying scientist can order stem cells from these labs.

Creating Stem Cell Lines

When a laboratory creates embryonic stem cells from one inner cell mass, and the cells grow longer than six to twelve months, that collection can be called an embryonic stem cell line. A stem cell line is created through a process that begins with the isolation of the thirty or so cells of the inner cell mass of the four- or five-day-old blastocyst. The cells are placed onto a laboratory dish that contains a feeder cell layer to provide nutrients to allow the cells to multiply. (Originally, this culture was made up of embryonic mouse cells. Today, some newer stem cell lines are grown in other ways to prevent mouse molecules and viruses from contaminating the stem cells.)

After they are isolated and placed on the feeder cells in culture dishes, the cells from the inner cell mass quickly fill the lab dish, and, when they do, they are separated and transferred to other lab culture dishes in a process called subculturing. Within six months, the original thirty cells yield millions of embryonic stem cells—a new stem cell line.[5]

Scientists who want to use federal funding for their research may go to the National Institutes of Health Human Embryonic Stem Cell Registry for approved stem cell lines. The lines are available from several different laboratories around the world. In October 2005, the NIH awarded $16.1 million to Wisconsin's WiCell Research Institute to establish a National Stem Cell Bank to consolidate many of the stem cell lines in one location, maintain quality control, and reduce researchers' costs for cells. It also set aside $9.6 million for two Centers of Excellence in Translational Human Stem Cell Research to bring together stem cell and disease experts. The centers will be based at the University of California at Davis and Northwestern University.[6]

Researchers who choose to fund their work with private or state money are free to use other stem cell lines. The International Society for Stem Cell Research (ISSCR) Web site lists about eighty stem cell lines that are "characterized," or scientifically analyzed, at more than a dozen laboratories worldwide.[7] (The ISSCR is an independent, nonprofit organization made up of scientists and stem cell research advocates.) Labs in the United States on that list include Harvard University, the Reproductive Genetics Institute in Chicago, and the University of California at San Francisco.

The stem cells available at Harvard were created in 2003 by stem cell researcher Douglas Melton as part of an effort by the Howard Hughes Medical Institute, the Juvenile Diabetes Research Foundation, and Harvard to encourage embryonic stem cell research. Melton and his colleagues were very careful not to use any federal funds to develop the seventeen lines, going so far as to use a separate room, supplies, and equipment for the research. (Melton has since isolated an additional eleven stem cell lines.) By December 2004, Melton's lab had shipped out more than three hundred samples, mainly to scientists overseas.[8]

Melton's work "touched off a wave of excitement" in the scientific community and attracted national attention to the issue of stem cell research and to Harvard, which in March 2004 announced the establishment of the Harvard Stem Cell Institute.[9] The institute is using stem cells to research cures for diabetes, neurological diseases, blood diseases, cardiovascular diseases, and musculoskeletal diseases. One of the goals of the institute is to create stem cells using nuclear transfer.[10]

Melton and fellow researcher Kevin Eggan have requested permission from Harvard officials to use nuclear transfer techniques to create and investigate what they call a "disease line" of embryonic stem cells—cells derived from people afflicted with a specific disease, such as diabetes. A top Harvard official approved of the researchers' plans in March 2005.[11]

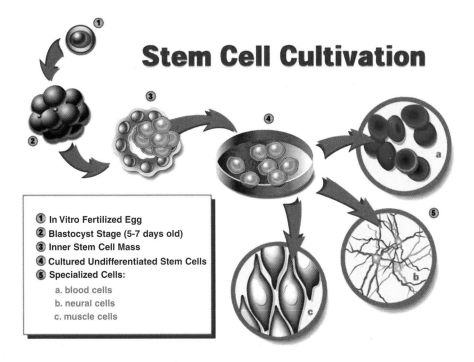

Stem Cell Cultivation

① In Vitro Fertilized Egg
② Blastocyst Stage (5-7 days old)
③ Inner Stem Cell Mass
④ Cultured Undifferentiated Stem Cells
⑤ Specialized Cells:
   a. blood cells
   b. neural cells
   c. muscle cells

This illustration from the University of Wisconsin shows how embryonic stem cells are derived from fertilized eggs less than one week old.

Making Use of Human Embryonic Stem Cell Lines

One of the biggest challenges to embryonic stem cell research is figuring out how to coax stem cells to differentiate into specialized cells. Using undifferentiated embryonic stem cells in live organisms is risky: Research has shown that when pluripotent stem cells are injected into specially bred mice that lack a healthy immune system, the cells generate teratomas, tumors made up of a mixture of different cell types.[12] Teratoma is taken from the Greek word *teraton*, which means "monster," because of stem cells' ability to create bizarre tumor formations. When University of Wisconsin researcher James Thomson injected his new stem cells under the skin of mice, he observed tumors that included bone, gut, muscle, and brain cells.[13]

Years of laboratory experimentation have established a few

basic "recipes" scientists can follow to direct the development of embryonic stem cells. Scientists know that all of the cells in a human body, and all the cells in one stem cell line, contain the same twenty-five thousand to thirty thousand genes. Many genes are active in all types of cells, but certain genes are active only in certain types of cells. For example, only those genes that define and control a heart muscle cell are actually active in a heart muscle cell.

Scientists can activate certain types of genes in human embryonic stem cells in two ways: They can insert certain genes that will direct the cell to develop a specific way, or they can add hormones and other growth factors to the cells' culture to prompt certain genes to "switch on" and produce a specific type of cell.[14] Knowing how to activate a cell's own genes to produce a certain specialized cell would be a dramatic leap forward in the field of cell biology. It could enable scientists to create safe replacement cells for patients with specific illnesses, such as Parkinson's disease. (In Parkinson's, the brain cells that help control muscle movement are destroyed.)[15] Inserting cells into an individual in the hope that the cells can repair, rescue, or replace damaged ones is called "regenerative medicine" and "cell-based therapy." Bone marrow transplant is a type of regenerative medicine. Embryonic stem cells are not yet used in any type of therapy. Some think the hope that they will be is hype. Others are convinced that they are the future of regenerative medicine.

Many scientists are finding that not all human embryonic stem cell lines are alike—some are much better at becoming heart cells, for example, than nerve cells. "When you are trying

> **When a lab creates embryonic stem cells from one inner cell mass, and the cells grow longer than six to twelve months, that collection is called an embryonic stem cell line.**

to do research, you look for every advantage you can," Leonard Zon, founder and director of the Stem Cell Program at Children's Hospital in Boston, told *The New York Times* in an August 2004 summary of the state of stem cell science. "Some embryonic stem cell lines make particular tissues better than others."[16] Zon is also a Howard Hughes Medical Institute Investigator and a member of the Harvard Medical School faculty.

Research Progress Using Animals

Scientists have made some progress in figuring out how certain hormones and other stimuli can prompt embryonic stem cells to create several specialized cell types. They have also found ways to find and extract from a stem cell culture dish those stem cells that for some reason have spontaneously differentiated into what appears to be a certain type of cell. Scientists are now using these more specialized stem cells in experiments to see if they function like a normal cell inside a living animal. Most of these experiments are done on rats or mice, but some use pigs or apes, whose biological systems are more similar to that of humans.

Spinal cord injury. In one of the most widely publicized research accomplishments in the past few years, paralyzed rats given injections of engineered embryonic stem cells not only regained movement after treatment, they were also able to walk.[17]

Scientist Hans Keirstead, of the University of California at Irvine and the Reeve-Irvine Research Center, coaxed embryonic stem cells to create progenitor cells that would produce only oligodendrocytes, a certain type of brain cell.[18] The researchers then inserted the cells into rats with spinal cord injuries. (Oligodendrocytes form the substance myelin, which insulates the "wiring" in the brain and the spinal cord that sends brain signals to other cells in the body. In spinal cord injury, if the myelin is damaged, and the signaling impaired, paralysis results.) Rats receiving the transplants within seven days of their injury regained the ability to walk within weeks of the treatment.

Federally approved human embryonic stem cell lines were used in the research, which was undertaken at the Reeve-Irvine Research Center.

Keirstead's accomplishment has drawn the attention of many other researchers not only because of its therapeutic potential, but also because in the process he developed a method to turn human embryonic stem cells into highly pure progenitor cells. (Recall that a progenitor cell is a "daughter" cell of an undifferentiated stem cell. The progenitor cell divides to create two very specific types of cells.) These highly pure progenitor cells are very valuable for research and therapy because contamination with embryonic stem cells could lead to teratoma (benign tumor) formations. Much research must be done to assure the treatment is absolutely safe, for, as Keirstead said in an interview following announcement of his results, "You don't want toenails growing in the brain."[19]

About eleven thousand Americans suffer a spinal cord injury every year, and four hundred-fifty thousand people in the United States live with sustained traumatic spinal cord injuries.[20]

"You've got a patient community out there that is in desperate need," Keirstead said. "If the treatment is safe, let's get it out there and try it."[21]

Type 1 diabetes. Another human ailment for which human embryonic stem cell research holds much promise is diabetes, in particular Type 1 diabetes. Diabetes (Types 1 and 2) is a devastating, lifelong disease that afflicts about 18 million Americans.[22] Because Type 1 diabetes often strikes children, it was known for a long time as "juvenile diabetes," but since it can also develop in adulthood, it is now usually known as Type 1 diabetes.

Dr. Hans Keirstead, at the University of California at Irvine, leads a research team that is investigating stem cell differentiation. In their work, injured rats injected with the differentiated cells were cured of paralysis.

People develop Type 1 diabetes when their immune system has destroyed the beta cells of the pancreas, and as a result the pancreas no longer secretes the hormone insulin. (The pancreas is an organ behind the stomach. Beta cells are special cells inside the pancreas that make insulin.) Insulin controls how much sugar, or glucose, can enter the cells of the body. Without insulin, cells are deprived of fuel, and they cannot function normally. People with Type 1 diabetes are insulin-dependent for life, and they must monitor their glucose levels at all times or they risk severe complications such as blindness, amputation, heart disease, stroke, and kidney failure.[23]

Almost immediately after the University of Wisconsin researchers showed that it was possible to maintain human embryonic stem cells in the lab, one scientist in particular began an aggressive campaign to use human embryonic stem cells in diabetes research. Doug Melton, Howard Hughes Medical Institute investigator and Harvard professor of natural science, made it his goal to use this new technology to find a cure for diabetes for the millions of Americans, including his son, who live with Type 1 diabetes.[24] Melton's daughter has since been diagnosed with the condition as well.

"My first reaction was that I would rather die than have to support myself on insulin injections for the rest of my life," said Emma Melton, who has watched her younger brother manage life with diabetes since he was a baby. The disease was a surprise to everyone: There was no history of diabetes in either family. Emma must now also take up to six insulin injections a day, but she has not let diabetes slow her down. She plans to work for a cure for diabetes when she graduates from college—"if the disease is not already cured by then."[25]

To hasten research to find a cure for diabetes as well as other diseases, Doug Melton derived the seventeen new stem cell lines mentioned above. In addition, he helped drive the creation of the new Harvard Stem Cell Research Institute, which he now codirects.

In 2002, scientists at Stanford University advanced the field of diabetes research by creating cells from mouse embryonic cells that, when transplanted into diabetic mice, significantly reduced blood sugar and extended the lives of the mice.[26] When the researchers removed the grafted cells, the mice died.

In 2004, researchers in Korea reported that they were able to generate insulin-producing cells from human embryonic stem cells, though the insulin production was spontaneous and not in response to glucose.[27]

Also in 2004, Melton discovered an unexpected source of insulin-producing cells: the mature beta cells themselves.[28] It was the first time ever that mature cells were considered capable of making new cells—in other words, of acting like stem cells. The report was good news for diabetes patients who still have some mature beta cells, because it might be possible someday to coax those cells to replenish their bodies' lost insulin-producing cells.

"On the other hand," Melton said of the findings, "if Type 1 diabetics don't have any beta cells left, then these findings suggest that the only source of new beta cells is probably going to be embryonic stem cells, because there [do not] appear to be adult stem cells involved in regeneration."[29]

> **Knowing how to activate a cell's own genes to produce a certain specialized cell would be a dramatic leap forward in the field of cell biology.**

The results do not rule out the existence of adult stem cells that produce beta cells. Researchers are now investigating whether such cells exist or if there are other cells within the pancreas that can be triggered to behave like beta cells and produce insulin.

Heart tissue, eye cells, and cancer-seeking "missiles." Other research accomplishments reported in 2004 in embryonic stem cell research seemed to hold promise for future treatments for human heart disease, vision problems, and brain cancer.

Advanced Cell Technology, a private company in Massachusetts, reported finding a special type of eye cell spontaneously growing in some of their human embryonic stem cell cultures. These cells are known to play a lead role in the healthy functioning of the human eye. Without these cells, the eyes

Dr. Doug Melton, codirector of the Stem Cell Research Institute at Harvard, is working to find a cure for diabetes. He has also created seventeen new embryonic stem cell lines, which are now available to other researchers.

deteriorate, often resulting in the loss of vision. The company is conducting studies in large animals to see if transplanting the cells can help restore vision.[30]

When researchers in Israel observed heart cells beating in their human embryonic stem cell cultures, they took those cells from the culture and put them into a lab dish with rat heart cells, which beat at a different pace than human heart cells. Within a day, the cells beat at the same pace. To see if the heart cells could do the same in a large animal, they injected one hundred thousand of their embryonic stem cell-derived heart cells into pigs whose hearts were damaged and beat slower than usual. Eleven of the thirteen hearts soon returned to the faster heart rates.[31]

A researcher at the Burnham Institute in California used human embryonic stem cells in mice to seek and destroy a fatal form of brain cancer. Evan Snyder, professor and director of Burnham's Stem Cells and Regeneration Program, and his colleagues modified the stem cells so that they would make a certain molecule that is known to kill cancer cells. In his experiments, the cells migrated across the brain to the site of injury, as stem cells are known to do, produced the molecules, and cut the tumor size by an average of 50 percent, and in some cases nearly 70 percent. The researchers said that they hoped the treatment could be tried in humans soon. They were also careful to note that the technique could not remove a tumor on its own.[32]

Using stem cells as both carriers and producers of molecules like this that can serve as a medicine is one of the first ways stem cells might be used to treat human ailments, Snyder said, so long as the procedure proves to be safe. "All you are asking the stem cells to do is find the nasty bit, get rid of it, and not cause mischief along the way."[33]

Clinical Trials Years Away

When medical researchers think they have developed or found a promising treatment for a human disease or condition and would like to offer that treatment in the United States, they must first conduct research using animals as treatment subjects. If the experiments produce the desired results, the researchers seek FDA approval to enter it into what are called Phase I clinical trials. In general, in Phase I trials the treatment is given to healthy people who are closely monitored to determine the effects of the treatment. If Phase I trials are successful, which means that the effects are as predicted and no major side effects are observed, the researchers then initiate Phase II clinical trials, in which the treatment is given to people afflicted with the condition the researchers hope to treat. Many more patients are involved in Phase III trials, which are often arranged so that researchers can compare the treatment to a known one. If a treatment does well in Phase III, the researchers may seek approval from the FDA to offer it to American consumers.[34]

As of January 2006, no therapies using human embryonic stem cells were listed as in the clinical trials stage—Phase I, II, or III—on the FDA clinical trials Web site.[35]

"Stem cell science remains in its infancy," researchers at the University of Wisconsin report. "It will likely be years at best before technologies emerging from embryonic stem cells find clinical application."[36]

Scientific Hurdles

As is the case with adult stem cells, there are issues that must be resolved before the work of embryonic stem cell researchers can yield potential future therapies—if in fact it ever does. For example, at present it is thought that embryonic stem cells cannot be used in patients unless they have been set along a path to become a specific type of cell. As James Thomson demonstrated at the University of Wisconsin, injecting an embryonic stem cell into a living organism produces a teratoma. As a matter of fact, this procedure—injecting undifferentiated stem cells into organisms and looking for teratomas—is one of the ways scientists test cells to find out if they are, indeed, stem cells.

Two other very important hurdles must be overcome before any treatment produced from human embryonic stem cell research could be considered for clinical trials.

First, researchers need to be absolutely sure that the cells they intend to transfer to patients are not contaminated by mouse cells from the feeder layers on which the human embryonic stem cells are grown or by viruses or bacteria within these mouse cells. A panel of scientists and ethicists (people who study moral issues) convened in 2003 by Johns Hopkins Medicine issued a statement saying the human embryonic stem cell lines eligible for federal research dollars "are not suitable for use in future clinical trials" because they were grown on mouse feeder lines.[37] Two years later, researchers at the University of California at San Diego found that certain sugar molecules not present on human cells in the mouse cell membranes were becoming incorporated into the growing human embryonic stem cells. The study showed that the contamination is not toxic to the cells directly, but it would make those stem cells a target to the human body's immune system, which would consider those cells foreign—and destroy them.[38]

Secondly, any human embryonic stem cell transferred into a patient's body must be similar to the patient's own cells in order to be accepted by the patient's body. As mentioned above, as with organ transplants, if certain proteins on the transplanted cells' surface differ too greatly, the cells are rejected. Some scientists think that research using NT could help solve this problem of transplant rejection, as the therapeutic cells would express the patients' own genes and proteins and would not be recognized as "foreign" by the patient's immune system.

In the meantime, the charged debate about whether such work is ethical, and whether it should be allowed, continues. In addition, the question remains as to whether the promise of human embryonic stem cell research has been overblown. Is it hype? Or is it hope? There is one thing for certain as the discussion and the science proceed: In the words of the National Institutes of Health, the promise of embryonic stem cell research "is an exciting one, but significant technical hurdles remain that will only be overcome through years of intensive research."[39]

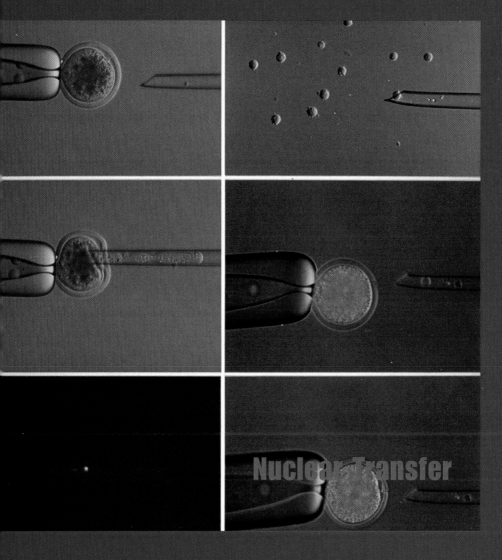

There is a popular scenario that is retold often in discussions about human embryonic stem cell research. It goes something like this: Imagine that you have suffered a heart attack and that your heart is gradually but surely deteriorating. Your doctor refers you to a specialist, who scrapes a skin cell from your arm and schedules an appointment for you in the operating room sometime within the next few weeks. At the appointed time you find your way to the hospital and, after a whiff of anesthesia, receive a transplant of custom-made, healthy heart stem cells—cells created from the combination of your very own DNA and a donor egg cell—that immediately find their way to your heart. Your doctor has assured you that these new cells will not be rejected by your body's immune system. They are, after all, your cells.

This scenario is, at present, purely fiction. It illustrates, though, one of the reasons why some stem cell research advocates and scientists would like to use nuclear transfer to create human embryonic stem cells.

Stem cells created through NT are genetically identical to the "parent" cell. If researchers could figure out how to direct stem cells to create specialized cells, then, theoretically, medical experts could someday create custom-made repair kits for each and every patient. Tissue and organ rejection would be a thing of the past.

But some ethicists, religious groups, and others are deeply troubled. Are those masses of cells created through NT simply a means for creating embryonic stem cells, proliferating in a laboratory culture dish, or are they human embryos, created through a new scientific procedure, but deserving of moral status? What is more, are those cells created in the lab, from which your doctor will harvest tailor-made stem cells, embryonic clones of "you"?

What Is Nuclear Transfer?

Nuclear transfer is a laboratory technique in which the nuclear material—the DNA—of one cell is transferred to an enucleated egg cell (one from which the DNA has been removed). The egg is then placed in a culture dish and coaxed to grow by electrical or chemical stimulation. If all goes well, the egg rapidly divides, following the genetic directions of the transferred DNA, and in time it generates a blastocyst. If the nuclear material that is introduced into the egg is from a somatic cell—any cell in the body except an egg or sperm cell—the process is called somatic cell nuclear transfer (SCNT). Much of the debate about using nuclear transfer to create human embryonic stem cells has focused on two different possible uses for the cells produced. One of these uses is called "reproductive cloning." The other is "therapeutic cloning."

Cloning is a term that scientists have used for many years to refer to a process for creating duplicates of biological material. It is the creation of single or multiple copies of a cell, tissue, plant, or animal.[1] The genetic material of the copycat entities is identical to that of the original entity.

Many types of cloning are commonly used in science and in industry. Cloning is used to create new drugs, grow useful bacteria in the laboratory, and produce new plants that are resistant to disease.[2] Insulin, for example, an important protein that diabetics use to control their glucose levels, is produced in large quantities by genetically modified and cloned bacteria.[3]

> Are those masses of cells created through nuclear transfer simply a means for creating embryonic stem cells, or are they human embryos deserving of moral status?

When people think of cloning, they usually think of reproductive cloning, which is the creation of a genetic copy of another organism. Reproductive cloning gained international attention after the February 1997 report of the birth of Dolly, the famous sheep in Scotland who was the world's first cloned mammal. Dolly was developed from the DNA of a single cell scraped from a sheep's udder, not from the union of a ewe's egg and a ram's sperm. Her creators, scientists at the Roslin Institute in Edinburgh, created her by inserting the DNA from that udder cell into an unfertilized, enucleated egg.[4]

Producing a cloned creature is not as easy as it sounds. Of the 277 genetically manipulated eggs that the Roslin scientists created, only twenty-nine produced embryos that appeared normal. All were implanted into surrogate Scottish Blackface ewes, but only one embryo—the one that became Dolly—grew to full term.[5] Since Dolly's birth, cattle, pigs, rabbits, goats, mice, cats, horses, and other sheep have been cloned. Snuppy, the world's first cloned puppy, was introduced in 2005.[6]

Experience with animals has shown that clones are in very poor health their entire lives. Many have birth defects. Some researchers think cloned organisms cannot develop properly because "old" DNA is used. According to one expert who has studied cloning for more than a decade, there is no such thing as a normal clone because the genes that are needed for a cell to behave like an embryo and begin development are "turned off" in the adult cell. During reproductive cloning, the cells' genes are reprogrammed by the egg. Some of the instructions are turned on, and others are turned off. This reprogramming enables the blastocyst to grow, but it is not the same as that in a normal embryo, in which the turning on and off of different genes at just the right moment is like a carefully orchestrated ballet.[7]

Dolly was euthanized on February 14, 2003, following complications from lung disease. It is speculated that she aged prematurely.[8]

Experts agree that human reproductive cloning should not be allowed—for both ethical and scientific reasons. In an article on the Web site of the International Society for Stem Cell Research, researcher Richard Mollard, of Australia's Monash University, said the very notion of using somatic cell nuclear transfer to create an adult human clone is "opposed adamantly by a vast majority of scientists, doctors, and the general public at large."[9]

The InterAcademy Panel (IAP), a prestigious organization that represents science academies from nations around the world, issued the following statement on human cloning in September 2003: "Some countries have already banned the

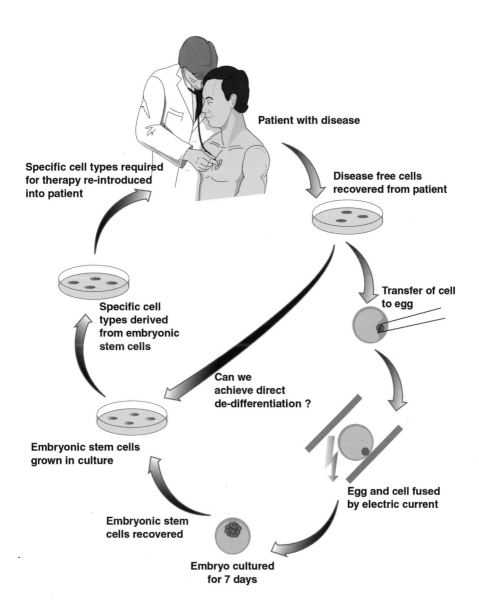

Patient with disease

Specific cell types required for therapy re-introduced into patient

Disease free cells recovered from patient

Specific cell types derived from embryonic stem cells

Transfer of cell to egg

Can we achieve direct de-differentiation ?

Embryonic stem cells grown in culture

Egg and cell fused by electric current

Embryonic stem cells recovered

Embryo cultured for 7 days

This diagram, provided by the Roslin Institute, illustrates the proposed use of nuclear transfer to create possible new stem cell therapies.

reproductive cloning of humans. We urge all other countries to introduce and support appropriate regulations to ensure that reproductive cloning is subject to a universal ban."[10] Sixty-seven IAP academies in October 2004 urged the United Nations to ban human reproductive cloning—but to allow therapeutic cloning for research purposes.[11]

In the United States, several highly regarded scientific organizations have called for a policy that would outlaw human reproductive cloning yet allow therapeutic cloning. These groups include the Coalition for the Advancement of Medical Research, an organization made up of 125 patient groups, scientific societies, and academic institutions, and the National Academies. (These consist of the National Academy of Sciences, National Academy of Engineering, Institute of Medicine, and the National Research Council. They are private, nonprofit institutions that provide science, technology, and health policy advice under a Congressional charter.)

Therapeutic Cloning

Dolly's creation stunned the world not only because she was the first cloned mammal, but also because of the new scientific feat used to create her. For the very first time, a totipotent stem cell—one capable of producing every cell in an organism—was produced from the genetic material of a mammal's adult body cell. Some medical researchers speculated that this technique, the cloning of somatic cells, might someday be used to create replacement cells, or maybe even organs, from a patient's very own skin cells. Researchers refer to this process as "therapeutic cloning."

Just as with reproductive cloning, therapeutic cloning begins with nuclear transfer. A somatic cell's nuclear material is transferred to an egg cell from which the DNA has been removed. In therapeutic cloning, though, the blastocyst that develops is not implanted in a uterus, as is the case in reproductive cloning.

Instead, the embryonic stem cells from the inner cell mass are isolated and transferred to a culture dish, where they grow and create a stem cell line. Each cell in the line contains the DNA of the "parent" somatic cell. These are the cells that some people hope may be of use someday for stem cell therapies.

Researchers at the Whitehead Institute in Massachusetts published results of an experiment done with mice in 2002 that demonstrated that therapeutic cloning may prove useful to treat disease.

The scientists removed a cell from the tail of a mouse that could not fight off infections. (Its immune system was nonfunctional because of a genetic defect.) The nuclear material of the cell was then transferred to an enucleated mouse egg, and the egg was stimulated to grow. When the egg reached the blastocyst stage, the scientists extracted the embryonic stem cells and carefully set about "correcting" the genetic flaw that they knew to be the root of the mouse's problems. They then coaxed the corrected stem cells to make blood cells, and they carefully injected the cells into their sick mouse. Remarkably, the mouse was cured.[12]

"We know a tremendous amount about mouse embryonic stem cells and how to culture and differentiate them," observed George Daley, who conducted the experiment in 2002 with Rudolf Jaenisch, professor at the Whitehead Institute at the Massachusetts Institute of Technology. "But for now, our understanding of how to do the same in human embryonic stem cells is much more primitive. . . . I'm sure there are challenges that we don't even know yet."[13]

Some people think that the first treatments that may evolve from these studies will be cell-based therapies, in which nuclear transfer will be used to produce stem cells genetically matched for each patient. After being coaxed to become specialized replacement cells, the stem cells would be injected into the patient's body to replace dead or diseased cells.[14] Some think nuclear transfer might someday be used to generate entire organs, but experts point out that organs are complex structures, and, at present, it is not possible to create a laboratory culture or setting that could provide the conditions needed for a sophisticated organ to grow.

The most immediate use for these cells would be for basic research into the origin of specific types of disease. As with treatments that may arise from research with conventional embryonic stem cells, the technical issues, such as how to direct a stem cell to create a specific type of specialized cell, need to be solved before possible proposed treatments can move from laboratory to the clinic. According to Jaenisch, "There are no indications at present that these represent formidable problems that will resist relatively rapid solution."[15]

From Dolly to Korea: Advances and News in Nuclear Transfer

The news of the birth of Dolly, the world's first cloned animal, was followed by many other "firsts" in the growing field of nuclear transfer and stem cell research. Some of these reports were startling:

- In January 1998, not quite a year after news of Dolly's birth, Richard Seed, a physicist from Riverside, Illinois, announced that he and a team of doctors planned to open a clinic to clone human beings for infertile couples.[16] (As of May 2006, the clinic had not materialized, and Seed had not produced a clone.)

- In March 2000, the Scottish research team that created Dolly announced that it had created five piglets through nuclear transfer techniques. They said they would next research ways that this technique could be used to create genetically modified pigs whose organs could be accepted by the human immune system. The process of inserting

The scientists who developed the technique known today as nuclear transfer used frog eggs of the North American leopard frog, *Rana pipiens*, in their research. They used a pipette, which is a very small tube, to suction a nucleus from a cell. They then inserted the nucleus into an enucleated egg.

animal organs or parts into humans, or vice versa, is called xenotransplantation. The scientists later decided not to do this research. The thought of xenotransplantation sparked much debate and raised a number of concerns, such as fear that pig virus may cross species into humans and create devastating new human illnesses.[17] Many were concerned about introducing so many human cells, and possibly human traits, into animals, especially if the animals were allowed to breed.

- In November 2001, scientists at Advanced Cell Technology reported that they had cloned human embryos, not to reproduce human beings, but to create a new source of stem cells for disease research.[18] The cloned embryos stopped growing after a few cell divisions, producing blastocysts made up of fewer than six cells each. The researchers used two techniques to develop the clones: nuclear transfer and *parthenogenesis*, a process through which an ordinary, unfertilized egg cell is stimulated to begin dividing. A year later, the ACT scientists reported that they had stimulated unfertilized monkey eggs to grow, and, what is more, they had extracted embryonic stem cells from one of those developing eggs.[19]

- In 2002, ACT scientists reported that they had created a stem cell line from cloned cow embryos, and that they had used the stem cells to grow functioning, miniature kidney-like "units" that were then successfully transplanted into adult cows.[20] The research was notable because the results suggested that stem cells created through NT may not trigger an immune reaction in patients who received the cells as transplanted tissues or organs.[21]

- In March 2004, a South Korean research team led by Woo Suk Hwang, of Seoul National University, reported in *Science* that they had produced the world's first human embryonic stem cell line from cloned human embryos.[22] The news won Hwang international attention. His accomplishment was heralded as an important milestone for stem cell science.

- In May 2005, Hwang and his research team published another groundbreaking paper, this time reporting they had created eleven new stem cell lines that were genetic matches to patients who had a variety of conditions and diseases. This was exciting news because research using disease-specific cells could shed light on inherited diseases and offer hope for those afflicted with such conditions.

The South Koreans credited their work, in part, to a new, highly efficient cloning method that used an average of only seventeen eggs for each stem cell line.[23]

- In December 2005 and January 2006, scandal shocked the stem cell science research community when Hwang, under mounting evidence that the results were fabricated, asked to have his 2005 paper withdrawn and resigned from South Korea's World Stem Cell Hub. Seoul National University immediately undertook a thorough investigation and quickly concluded that both of Hwang's research reports were bogus.[24] Hwang apologized for publishing false data, but maintained that he was duped by junior researchers.[25]

Creating Cells, Controversy, and Debate

When Hwang's 2004 paper first rolled off the press, and no one had reason to doubt his accomplishment, debate about what should and should not be allowed in stem cell research intensified.

A noted medical ethics professor pointed out the moral dilemma that such technology presented: "I think the big question is: If you make this kind of a thing in a dish, have you created human life?" said Arthur Caplan, medical ethicist and director of the University of Pennsylvania's Center for Bioethics, shortly after the March 2004 news made headlines. "Can you make something that people have strong moral views about in terms of destroying it, in order to benefit other people?"[26]

When the President's Council on Bioethics addressed the issue, they found they could not agree on how to advise President Bush on the ethics of cloning for biomedical research. According to their report:

> All parties to the debate have concerns vital to defend, vital not only to themselves but to all of us. No human being and no society can afford to be callous to the needs of suffering humanity, or cavalier about the treatment of nascent human life, or indifferent

to the social effects of adopting one course of action rather than another.[27]

Alternative Sources of Embryonic Stem Cells

Several alternative sources for embryonic stem cells have been suggested in the past few years as a way to avoid the ethical issues involved in creating and destroying embryos.

Parthenotes. When Advanced Cell Technology created human embryos by stimulating unfertilized human eggs to grow completely on their own, they introduced into the stem cell debate an alternative method to obtain human embryonic stem cells. This method is called parthenogenesis, from the Greek word for "virgin birth." Female insects such as honeybees, flies, and ants often reproduce without male fertilization, as do some lizards, birds, snakes, and fish, under certain conditions. Mammals, however, do not naturally reproduce in this manner: It takes both female and male reproductive cells to produce an embryo. Mammal egg cells were first made to grow through parthenogenesis in vitro, or in a laboratory culture, in 1939.[28]

When an egg is stimulated to grow through parthenogenesis, it produces a "parthenote," a multicelled structure that looks like a developing blastocyst. Most mammal parthenotes do not survive for long. Mouse parthenotes are known to have survived the longest, about thirty days.[29]

Like cloning, parthenogenesis is not as simple as it sounds. The ACT scientists who created human blastocysts through this process reported exposing twenty-two unfertilized human egg cells to chemicals known to prompt cell division. After five days, only six of those eggs had grown into what appeared to be blastocysts. None of the blastocysts contained an obvious inner cell mass, the cells from which scientists derive embryonic stem cell lines.[30]

Some researchers think that parthenotes might produce abnormal tissue because they lack genetic material from a male.[31] A normal cell contains chromosomes inherited from both the female egg and the male sperm.

Some think parthenotes may provide an ethical alternative to obtain stem cells, as parthenotes cannot survive much beyond the blastocyst stage. Others disagree.

Biological artifacts. One scientist has proposed the creation of "biological artifacts"—cells created using nuclear transfer and genetic engineering that contain human embryonic stem cells but that are not organized enough to be considered human.

A number of female insects, such as honeybees, can reproduce without males, though mammals cannot.

This would require a discussion, though, about what parts of a human embryo make it "human."

Speaking to the President's Council on Bioethics in December 2004, William Hurlbut, a council member and consulting professor at Stanford University, said scientists could genetically alter reproductive cells to create "disorganized and non-functional masses" that contain stem cells. Teratomas, or tumors made of cells from all three germ layers of the human body, are examples of cells that for some unknown reason have begun specializing in a disorganized manner. Scientists could create such stem cell-producing entities by removing part of a cell's genetic code, Hurlbut said. Such masses already exist in nature in the form of ovarian cancers, which begin when an egg cell in a woman's ovary spontaneously begins dividing.

Hurlbut told the council:

> We raise the possibility that, using the technique of nuclear transfer, it may be possible to produce embryonic stem cells within a limited cellular system that is biologically and morally akin to a complex tissue culture and thereby bypass moral concerns about the creation and disruption of human embryos.

He called the proposed method "alternate nuclear transfer," and he prefaced his comments by saying the idea is "a concept, an approach to a problem."[32]

Cells from expired embryos. Two doctors from Columbia University proposed another solution. They suggested that stem cells be taken from embryos created in IVF clinics that had died; that is, after freezing and thawing, they had stopped growing after the eight-cell stage (meaning that they could never develop into a baby). An experiment with tadpoles had shown that even though the organism had stopped developing, a single cell from the cell mass could proliferate in a culture dish just as stem cells do in stem cell line cultures.[33]

These salvaged embryonic stem cells could provide society with a noncontroversial source of stem cells that "maintains respect for human dignity and can advance biomedical research," said the doctors, Howard Zucker and Don Landry.[34] Just as with organ donation, in which organs are taken from a person who has died and donated to a living patient, these cells, taken from a deceased embryo, could be donated to research.

Extracting single cells. Yet another suggested method proposes that one or two embryonic stem cells could be taken from a normal, healthy human embryo. The cells could then be used to create a stem cell line. (This procedure is currently done to evaluate whether an IVF embryo has a serious inherited disease.) Some think this procedure puts embryos at too great a risk. In addition, a stem cell line cannot be reliably generated from a single cell.[35]

The Debate Continues

Some people object to all of these proposed methods because they believe these procedures—like nuclear transfer—create and destroy human life.

Some scientists object to these and other proposed methods because they think that each has its own set of confounding scientific problems and ethical issues. They also think that these proposals are a distraction from the debate at the center of embryonic stem cell research: whether it is justifiable to use human embryos for this purpose.[36]

The answer to that question, increasingly, is not only a matter of personal opinion. It is a matter of which state in the union the stem cell research is proposed. Some states ban any work that destroys human embryos and threatens those who violate the ban with imprisonment. Some states allow it. Some encourage stem cell research, and they have set aside millions of dollars to support it.

5 Public Policy

It was in the mid-1990s when Wisconsin biologist James
Thomson decided to try to isolate and maintain human embryonic stem cells in the lab—a feat that no one had yet
accomplished. After thinking long and hard about the status of
the embryo, and deciding, in the end, that discarding an
embryo was not any better than using it in research, he began
looking for funding to get his work under way.[1] The federal
government at that time did not provide grant money for such
research, so Thomson accepted financial support from the
Wisconsin Alumni Research Foundation and Geron

Corporation, a biotechnology firm based in Menlo Park, California. Thomson set himself up in a lab off the University of Wisconsin campus—he did not want to jeopardize federal funding for other university research projects—and he quickly got to work.[2]

Today, researchers who would like to conduct experiments involving human embryonic stem cells do not have to set up separate laboratories off campus—as long as they agree to use only those embryonic stem cell lines that were created before August 9, 2001, the date the Bush administration policy went into effect. Scientists who would like to use stem cells from other stem cell lines—or derive stem cells themselves—do need to take whatever steps are necessary to separate that research from work on approved stem cell lines. This is because NIH rules prohibit the use of federal dollars to investigate stem cell lines created after August 9, 2001. Scientists are very careful, for example, not to use equipment purchased with federal dollars when conducting research on the new lines.

In addition to separating the research, scientists who want to use the newer stem cell lines, or to derive human embryonic stem cells themselves, need to find an alternative to government funding. Some have turned to private companies for support. Many businesses are willing to provide cash for research in exchange for the rights to any invention or process that may come of the research. Lately, many scientists are also finding a new source of financial support—funding from their home state treasury.

Nowhere is support for stem cell research greater than in the state of California.

Californians Invest $3 Billion

California voters in November 2004 approved a ballot initiative to invest $3 billion over the next ten years in human embryonic stem cell research. That is $300 million a year every year for a decade.

"This is going to be the stem cell center of the world, not just the country," said Evan Snyder, of the Burnham Institute, shortly after the vote on the initiative, which was called Proposition 71 on the California ballot.[3]

Backers of the proposition, which created the California Institute for Regenerative Medicine, hope the investment will create jobs and generate handsome returns. The institute will dole out funding as needed to California hospitals, medical schools, and universities that advance stem cell research—research that planners hope will someday help California reduce its health care costs by billions of dollars.[4]

California law bans "cloning to create babies." The organizers of Proposition 71 promised in their campaign information that they would maintain strict controls to make sure that all research that is funded abides by the law and is carefully reviewed so that unqualified businesses and scientists do not take advantage of the system. The institute's organizers—scientists, politicians, medical organizations, and private citizens—also promised that all human embryonic stem cell research would "involve fertilized eggs from fertility clinics that would otherwise be destroyed or other donated eggs that are provided with the fully informed consent of the donors." Also, they said that stem cells would be derived only from blastocysts in the first twelve days of development.[5]

"California has always been a pioneer," said Governor Arnold Schwarzenegger in throwing his support behind the vote in October 2004. "We daringly led the way for the high-tech industry, and now voters can help ensure we lead the way for the bio-tech industry."[6]

Critics of the plan say there is no evidence that stem cell research will ever produce cures for human ailments, and that the $3 billion investment is a giant gamble.

"Why is the state with the lowest credit rating and the highest debt cost in the country responsible now for borrowing money to pay for dubious research for the rest of the world?" Academy Award-winning director Mel Gibson asked in opposing Proposition 71. Gibson, a vocal opponent of the initiative, said the campaign to persuade Californians to vote for Proposition 71 was pushed by companies that stand to gain from it.[7]

A year after Proposition 71 passed, a group of California citizens filed a lawsuit challenging the legality of the institute. A California Superior Court judge in April 2006 ruled that the institute was within the letter of the law.

When the California voters back in 2004 approved of the proposition, officials and scientists from research organizations across the country feared a "brain drain" of their most talented medical scientists. Would their researchers leave home for the more lucrative stem cell research environment in California?

"We here in Massachusetts are not going to take this lying down," said Harvard's George Daley shortly after the vote. "We're going to have to work extra hard to make sure we don't lose our best junior scientists to California."[8]

States Pressed to Address the Issue

California was not the first state to show interest in allowing— and funding—stem cell research. New Jersey in early 2004 legalized human embryonic stem cell research and established the Stem Cell Institute of New Jersey, a new state-of-the-art research building for both adult and human embryonic stem cell research. By July 2005, New Jersey had expended $23.6 million for stem cell research and earmarked $10.5 million for facilities and research in the following year.[9] In 2005, Governor Richard Codey proposed that the state add $380 million to the effort. The plan called for more than half of that sum to be generated from a bond issue that would have to be approved by New Jersey voters. As of April 2006, a new, similar plan had

When Dr. James Thomson of the University of Wisconsin was working to be the first to isolate human embryonic stem cells in the lab, he received funding from outside groups and worked off campus so his research did not jeopardize federal funding for the university.

emerged, and the New Jersey Legislature was considering several bills that addressed stem cell research facilities and grants funding. The retooled plan was supported by New Jersey's new governor, Jon S. Corzine.

"We have the scientists, we have the research industries, and we have the commitment to make New Jersey an international center of stem cell excellence," Codey said in his January 2005 State of the State address. "But it will not happen by itself. It will not happen without actions to match our words."[10]

Wisconsin Governor Jim Doyle announced in November 2004 a plan to invest $750 million over the next several years in embryonic stem cell research and other biotechnology, $500 million of which would be set aside for new facilities and direct research support for scientists at the University of Wisconsin-Madison.[11]

Many other state legislators have visited—and in some cases revisited—their policies and funding arrangements for stem cell research. In 2005, Connecticut Governor Jodi Rell signed into law an act that provides $100 million for stem cell research through the next ten years. In Massachusetts, which is home to Harvard Stem Cell Institute, state lawmakers in 2005 overturned the governor's veto of a bill that permits the derivation of embryonic stem cell lines and nuclear transfer.[12]

"A new kind of red and blue state [Republican versus Democrat] division is developing over stem cell research," said Daniel Perry, president of the Coalition for the Advancement of Medical Research, an umbrella organization of more than one hundred groups that support human embryonic stem cell research. "In some states, you're a hero and get state funding. In others, you're threatened with prison."[13]

At present there is no federal law that prohibits research with human embryonic stem cells, but several bills have been introduced into Congress.

Before 2001

Some people mistakenly think that the Bush administration stem cell research policy for the first time restricted human embryonic stem cell research. Actually, the policy for the very first time allowed the use of federal funds for the creation of stem cell lines.

Before the 2001 announcement, no federal funds could be used for work that created or destroyed human embryos. This was because in 1996 Congress approved an amendment affecting what types of research could be funded by the National Institutes of Health. (The NIH provides about $28 billion every year to researchers in the medical sciences.[14]) The Dickey Amendment, named after its sponsor, Representative Jay Dickey of Arkansas, prohibited using funds "for the creation of human embryos for research purposes or for research in which human embryos are destroyed."[15] The amendment has been added to legislation affecting NIH spending every year since. The language used in 2005 defines an embryo as "any organism" that is "derived by fertilization, parthenogenesis, cloning, or any other means. . . ."[16]

After the 1998 announcements that ushered in a new concept in laboratory science—human embryonic stem cells that could survive in a laboratory dish—both scientists and policy makers found they needed a better explanation as to what types of research the NIH would fund. Would the federal government fund the work of a researcher using these new stem cells that they had obtained from other laboratories—work that did not directly involve that researcher in the direct destruction to human embryos?

Federal officials decided funding could be provided because the cells involved "are not a human embryo within the statutory definition" of an organism—that is, something that when implanted into a uterus could develop into a human being.[17] The NIH published guidelines following this ruling. Funds could be used for research using stem cells derived from human embryos "that were created for the purposes of fertility treatment and were in excess of the clinical need of the individuals seeking treatment."[18] There were other provisions as well. One stated that funding would not be provided for research to derive stem cells using nuclear transfer. In other words, funding would be provided for work with stem cells from an established line, but not work that actually derived the stem cells and resulted in the destruction of an embryo. The guidelines were put on hold,

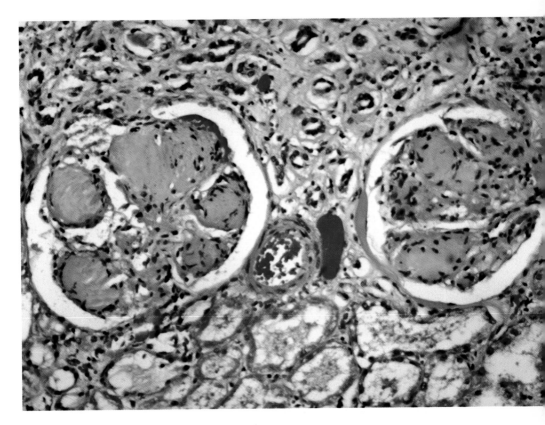

Diabetes is among the many diseases that scientists hope to fight with treatments arising out of stem cell research. Shown is a diseased kidney that has been damaged by diabetes.

though, when President George W. Bush came into office in 2000 and ordered a review of the situation.

In August 2001, President Bush reached a decision. Funding would be available, but only for stem cell lines already in use before August 9, 2001.[19] As of May 2006, those guidelines remain in place.

"The president's policy is working," wrote Tommy G. Thompson, then secretary of the U.S. Department of Health and Human Services, in *USA Today* in August 2004. Thompson mentioned that federal funding for embryonic stem cell research grew from zero in 2001 to $24.8 million in

2004, "with no cap on future funding." He also announced that as a result of intense interest "to further accelerate research in the field," the NIH was taking two new steps. First, it would create three Centers of Excellence in Translational Stem Cell Research, funded with $18 million over four years, to help scientists and doctors work together to cure human diseases. Second, it would create a National Embryonic Stem Cell Bank to provide scientists with a more convenient source of human embryonic stem cells that may be used in federally funded research.[20]

Not everyone agrees with Thompson's assessment of the policy. In April 2004, 206 members of the House of Representatives signed a letter to the president urging him to expand the number of stem cell lines. A few months later, 58 U.S. senators signed a similar letter. Also that year, 48 Nobel Prize recipients endorsed John Kerry's presidential candidacy, citing, among other things, Bush's "unwarranted restrictions on stem cell research."[21]

In May 2005, the House of Representatives passed a bill to expand federal funding for embryonic stem cell research. The bill, sponsored by Senators Arlen Specter, a Republican from Pennsylvania, and Tom Harkin, a Democrat from Iowa, allows the government to fund studies using IVF embryos in storage at fertility clinics, as long as the embryos are donated to science by the couples who created them. The bill is now on the docket of the U.S. Senate. President Bush has vowed to veto the bill if it is approved by Congress.

Many special interest groups are working to persuade senators why human embryonic stem cell research should be expanded so that more lines may be created—or why funding should continue to be restricted.

The American Association for the Advancement of Science (AAAS) weighed in on the matter in a letter to each senator in July 2005: "AAAS has stated that policy makers must reassess the Administration's August 2001 policy periodically 'so that changes must be made in order to realize to the fullest extent possible the benefits of this promising field of research,'" the letter said. "That time is now."[22]

International Policy

While the federal government and states within America debate the pros and cons of embryonic stem cell research, a few foreign nations with less restrictive policies are encouraging their stem cell researchers to press ahead.[23]

In October 2005, South Korea announced it would invest $6.5 million in a new World Stem Cell Hub. The hub would build on significant research already under way.[24]

Singapore launched "Biopolis," a $300 million science park focused on all types of biomedical science, including stem cell research.[25]

Britain became a world leader in human embryonic stem cell research in 2001 when it became the first country to legalize nuclear transfer. The country established a national organization that reviews all such stem cell research proposals, and it established a stem cell bank, through which it stores and distributes all stem cell lines in Britain free of charge.[26] In January 2005, the British government awarded its second license to clone.

"This is an important area of research and a responsible technology," said Suzi Leather, chairwoman of the Human Fertilization and Embryology Authority, the British agency that issues cloning licenses, when the agency awarded the country's first license to clone in 2004.[27]

Not every country, though, agrees that such work is a good investment. Germany, Austria, and Ireland all ban the destruction of human embryos to create stem cell lines.[28]

In March 2005, 84 of the 191 countries that are members of the United Nations (UN) voted to support a declaration urging all governments to ban human cloning, including the cloning of human embryos for stem cell research. Thirty-four nations voted against the declaration, and 37 abstained (were present but did not vote).[29] (The other 36 member countries were absent.) A declaration is not legally binding on member nations. The U.S. representative to the United Nations voted for the ban.

The United Kingdom's representative to the United Nations said it was a "shame" that the UN could not agree on a ban of reproductive cloning instead. Some countries, such as Britain, are very capable of strictly controlling therapeutic cloning, the official said, adding that the UN vote would not affect research in his country.[30]

The Business of Stem Cells

Some people wonder if stem cell science is a new form of technology that the United States should invest in if it hopes to keep up with other countries. If it does not, the theory goes, the United States will lose out on any financial gain that might come from the new technology.[31]

Some scholars say the simple rules of "supply and demand" will keep businesses in line with what society thinks is right or wrong because businesses will not create products made in ways that people find offensive. In other words, they will not invest their resources in creating a product that consumers might not want to buy because it represents the "scary edges of scientific potential," reported Debra Spar, a professor at Harvard Business School.[32]

But other people point out that thinking of human embryos—even human embryonic stem cells—as products is already very scary. Are companies or laboratories that sell human embryonic stem cells, or even adult stem cells, selling "human parts?"

Some people ask why couples who are willing to give their frozen, unwanted embryos to research must donate—and not sell—those embryos, especially when a biotech company might make a profit from that donation. Does U.S. policy favor a system that benefits business? Some people find such talk about buying and selling human cells very dehumanizing. They fear that by allowing human embryonic stem cells to be bought and sold, society is losing its respect for human life.

There is also a concern that nuclear transfer, which requires human egg cells, will exploit young women, especially those in other countries. Will women who are in unfortunate situations undergo egg harvesting procedures because they desperately need money? Will some women for whatever reason feel coerced to donate their egg cells?

At least one woman working in the laboratory of South Korea's stem cell researcher Woo Suk Hwang said she had donated eggs for Hwang's research under pressure from Hwang.[33] Other women in the research team reported they were asked to sign forms volunteering to donate their eggs.[34] A total of 2,061 eggs from one hundred twenty-nine females were collected from four hospitals and provided to Hwang's research team from November 2002 to November 2005.[35]

As of 2002, about one thousand scientists at thirty firms in the United States were involved in stem cell science. Spending on that work that year was estimated to be $208 million.[36]

The United States government in 2003 spent $190.7 million on adult stem cell research, and $24.8 million on human embryonic stem cell research.[37]

With so much public and private money invested in stem cell research, some think a new sector of the American economy is emerging. It may be an expenditure on research that does not get very far, or it may be a rewarding and wise investment. Either way, is the United States ready for the possibility of a stem cell "industry"?

Perhaps the only thing for certain in the controversy about whether human embryos should be used as a source for embryonic stem cells is that there will continue to be debate on this issue for a long time.

The core of the problem is this: Should a developing human egg cell be regarded as human, deserving of the same status as a baby who has already been born? Is it wrong to destroy such an entity to obtain stem cells, even if those cells will be used for lifesaving research? As long as embryonic stem cells are sought for research, people will ask these very difficult questions.

Opponents of human embryonic stem cell research argue that a blastocyst is a person no matter how or why it was created. Other people think there is a big difference between an embryo growing inside a mother and a blastocyst that is created in a culture dish, whether in an IVF clinic or a medical researcher's laboratory.

Scientific Advances Generate More Questions

While these basic questions about the status of the human embryo are at the heart of the debate, there are other equally difficult questions that have emerged as scientists have proposed alternative ways to obtain human embryonic stem cells. Policy makers, religious leaders, and others have had to ponder what it is, exactly, that makes a human embryo a human being. For example, as in the case of nuclear transfer, is the product of skin cell DNA and an enucleated human egg simply a mass of cells proliferating in a laboratory dish, producing an embryolike structure, or is it a unique human individual? Are cloned embryos different from normal embryos? Should we create an embryolike structure that contains stem cells but lacks the other parts it needs to develop and grow?

Many people turn to religion to help them form an opinion. Others who do not belong to a religious organization may take a stand based on other reasons—on what they think is right, humane, or just. Those opposed to using human embryos in stem cell research, for example, might ask why public tax dollars should be spent on something that many people oppose, whether it is wrong to meddle with nature, or if research like this might open the door to even more objectionable scientific "progress." Those who support human embryonic stem cell research might question whether the government should "legislate morality"—that is, make laws based on what a few people think is right. Some fear restrictions on research will hurt

American business interests or stifle the advance of scientific knowledge.

Religious Guidance

Those who turn to religious leaders for guidance might be surprised to find a vast difference of opinion as to what is right and wrong. Even within one faith, leaders often have widely differing views.

As with almost all of the world's governments, most religious leaders agree, in the very least, that any nuclear transfer technology that creates human embryos should not be used to create a child. To begin with, as science has shown, cloning is unsafe, both for the clone and for the surrogate mother. Beyond that, there are deep concerns about the purpose of doing this. The terms used to say this in various religious traditions are different, but there is a common concern about the extent to which humans are "co-creators" with God.[1] All religious traditions call for caution.

Some religious organizations believe that a human embryo is a full-fledged human being from the moment of its creation and as such deserves protection and respect. The largest and most outspoken among these is the Roman Catholic Church. Other groups that also take this position include the Eastern Orthodox Church, Southern Baptists, and Evangelical and Conservative Protestant churches, according to Cynthia B. Cohen, senior research fellow at the Kennedy Institute of Ethics at Georgetown University.[2]

Some religious groups hold that a "certain amount of development" is needed for a fertilized egg to have "person" status, and they do not object to human embryonic stem cell research so long as certain conditions are met. These religions include some mainline and liberal Protestant churches, Judaism, and some Islamic religious traditions. The General Synod of the United Church of Christ, which adopted a resolution, accepts cloning human embryos up to the fourteenth day of development, but strictly opposes implanting them.[3] It recently called on President Bush to release federal funds for embryonic stem cell research.[4]

It is often difficult to determine the position of a particular faith if it does not have one central authority. This is the case with many Protestant churches and Buddhism, for example. One scholar thinks Buddhists might accept the use of embryos in research because it might lead to self-understanding and enlightenment, but, on the other hand, it might violate a principle that prohibits harm. There is a wide diversity of views among Buddhists on this subject because Buddhism emphasizes the authoritative nature of personal intuition and opinion.[5]

A family says grace at Thanksgiving dinner. Different religious groups hold widely varying ideas about embryonic stem cell research.

Roman Catholic and Jewish religious representatives are often quoted in news stories about stem cell research because their beliefs represent both sides of the debate.

The Catholic perspective. Leaders of the Roman Catholic Church take the stance: "Life once conceived, must be protected with the utmost care."[6]

The late Pope John Paul II urged the President to "reject practices that devalue and violate human life at any stage from conception until natural death."[7] The Pope identified several activities, or "related evils," that he said have led society toward a "culture of death."[8] These "evils" include abortion, assisted reproductive technology (such as in vitro fertilization), and artificial contraceptives, for example. (Abortion is a procedure a woman may choose to undergo to end a pregnancy. Artificial contraceptives are devices men and women may use to prevent unwanted pregnancies.)

The Pontifical Academy for Life in August 2000 listed its objections to human embryonic stem cell research in a document called "Declaration on the Production and the Scientific and Therapeutic Use of Human Embryonic Stem Cells." The most significant point is that from the moment that an egg and sperm unite, that fertilized egg is a "human subject" with a unique identity and begins its own "coordinated, continuous and gradual development" beyond a simple mass of cells.[9] The academy also stated in that document that it is wrong to engage in nuclear transfer because it creates human embryos slated for destruction. It is also wrong to obtain and use embryonic stem cells from stem cell lines created by other scientists, according to the academy, because human embryos were destroyed to create those cell lines.[10]

There are some Roman Catholic theologians who say that a case can be made for embryonic stem cell research. They call for a return to a "centuries-old Catholic position that a certain amount of development is necessary in order for a conceptus [fertilized egg, embryo, or fetus] to warrant personal status."[11] However, this idea is counter to the current official church position.

"I think that we are still learning about the realities of what this entity, the embryo, is," said Margaret Farley, professor of Christian ethics at Yale University Divinity School, "and therefore we need to be open about its moral status."[12]

The Jewish perspective. For Jews, society's responsibility to preserve the life and health of other human beings is a very important moral obligation.

"Our bodies belong to God; we have them on loan during our lease on life," according to Rabbi Elliot Dorff, a prominent Conservative Jewish scholar who is rector and distinguished professor of philosophy at the University of Judaism in Los Angeles. "God, as owner of our bodies, can and does impose conditions on our use of our bodies. Among those is the requirement that we seek to preserve human life and health (*pikkuah nefesh*)." It

> **Research on embryonic stem cells has made policy makers, religious leaders, and others ponder the question of what it is, exactly, that makes a human embryo a human being.**

follows, Rabbi Dorff said, that individually and as a society, "we have a duty to seek to develop new cures for human diseases."[13]

Most Jewish scholars believe this moral obligation to take care of one's body and the health of others takes precedence over concerns for the very early embryo.[14]

"We both may, and should, take the steps necessary to advance stem cell research and its applications in an effort to take advantage of its great potential for human healing," Dorff stated in a 2002 document for the Rabbinical Assembly's Committee on Jewish Law and Standards. (The Rabbinical Assembly is an international association of conservative rabbis founded in 1901.) The assembly passed a resolution in April 2003 to "publicly advocate" and "support" human embryonic stem cell research for research and therapeutic purposes.[15]

Dorff wrote:

> We may and should engage in such research for two reasons: First, we have a duty to heal, and, as a corollary to that, to develop our means to heal; and second, genetic materials, including embryos, lack the status of a person or even part of a person. . . .[16]

According to the Talmud, an important collection of Jewish religious and civil laws, during the first forty days of gestation, or growth in the uterus, the embryo and fetus are considered as "simply water." Scholars think this definition was put in place by rabbis long ago who had observed that miscarriages up to that point looked like water.[17]

In July 2001, the Union of Orthodox Jewish Congregations of America and the Rabbinical Council of America jointly issued a letter to President Bush urging him to allow federal funding of embryonic stem cell research under "carefully crafted and well-monitored guidelines."[18] (The union serves as the central coordinating agency for many American and Canadian Orthodox Jewish congregations, which are the most conservative of Jewish tradition.)

Religion and Politics in a Democracy

What bearing should religious perspectives have on public policy? Some scholars say religious views are useful and important. Though religious leaders may disagree about what is right in stem cell research, the majority share common values that provide a foundation for a civil debate. These values include concerns about treating humans "as ends in themselves," about the possible abuse of power by some, and the need to treat the poor in a "just manner."[19]

By its very definition, a democratic government creates policy based on what the majority of its citizenship thinks is right.

President George W. Bush has been a strong opponent of embryonic stem cell research. He tried to satisfy both sides of the debate by limiting research to established stem cell lines.

Policy makers try to strike a balance between the pros and cons of an issue. President George W. Bush said he worked to find a middle ground between two competing interests in the stem cell research debate. Some people wonder, though, whether there should not be an "overriding" principle on the issue of stem cell research—one that has such moral force that it should be adopted as policy.[20] But if so, which principle should that be?

Some people strongly object to inserting religious views into national policy. In the words of Ronald Prescott Reagan, the former president's son who spoke at the 2004 Democratic National Convention, should the "theology of a few" determine American research policy, especially if that policy might "forestall the health and well-being of the many?"[21]

"As a citizen in a democracy where there are many competing views on issues like this one, to what extent am I obligated to try to insert my religiously informed moral view into law and public policy?" asked Ronald M. Green, professor and director of the Ethics Institute at Dartmouth University. "Surely not everything that my religion is deeply committed to must be imposed on others."[22]

It is one thing for the government to allow and oversee such research. It is another, though, to fund it with public money. Some people object to the use of tax dollars to pay for research they find immoral. Others think the federal government does not need the approval of each and every taxpayer for every research proposal or program that it funds.

Key Issues

The different arguments for and against human embryonic stem cell research are numerous and they can be overwhelming. It helps to separate the issues into categories. The following is a summary of some of the major arguments for and against the research:

The use of "spare" human embryos from IVF clinics
For:

- If IVF is acceptable, and unneeded frozen embryos are disposed of anyway, why not obtain embryonic stem cells from them for research?

- Embryos created in a laboratory are not the same as embryos created and growing within the human body. They are incapable of ever developing beyond the blastocyst stage unless they are implanted into a uterus.

- Because a fertilized egg can divide to produce more than one human embryo before the fourteenth day of development, how could a fertilized egg be considered a separate and distinct human individual with a soul?

- Adult stem cells hold promise, but they cannot take the place of human embryonic stem cells because adult stem cells are not found in every part of the body. In addition, adult stem cells are difficult to identify and isolate, and they are already somewhat specialized.

Against:

- An embryo is a human life, no matter its location or stage of development.

- There is no guarantee this research will lead to cures. There are many technical hurdles, such as how to get a stem cell to specialize into another type of cell. There is also a question as to whether these cells will function as desired inside the human body and if they are safe to use.

- Cell-based therapies and any other creations made with human embryonic stem cells from "spare" embryos may not be successful. These therapies may be rejected by a patient's body in the same way that transplanted organs sometimes are rejected.

- Research using adult stem cells should be pursued more aggressively because it does not present a moral dilemma.

The use of embryos, or embryolike structures, created through nuclear transfer, human embryo cloning, and parthenogenesis
For:

- Nuclear transfer creates cell masses, proliferating in a culture dish, not human embryos. Even if implanted into a human uterus, it is highly unlikely that such a mass could develop beyond the fetal stage.

- Nuclear transfer could be used to create cell-based therapies and someday possibly organs "tailor made" for each individual.

- Through human embryo cloning techniques, scientists can create disease-specific stem cells from patients with certain diseases. They could study these cells to better understand what causes these diseases, and possibly, in the future, treat these diseases through cell-based therapy.

Against:

- It is wrong to create an entity that is self-directed to grow into a human embryo just to destroy it later to harvest the stem cells within.

- All of these techniques require egg cells. This could create a demand for human eggs, which may possibly exploit women.

- In addition to DNA inside the nucleus, which is removed in some cloning processes, all egg cells contain other, inherited, DNA that is inside the cell's cytoplasm. This DNA may affect the resulting stem cells, and that may, in turn, affect whether a patient's body accepts or rejects tailor-made, cell-based therapies.

A Call for Supervision

Several ethicists have called for more federal monitoring of human embryonic stem cell research. They argue that such an important issue should not be left to each state to regulate, or to the free market system, in which businesses make decisions based on future profits. Such a patchwork of policy is currently the case with IVF and other types of assisted reproductive technologies, which have been going on for decades, subject to very little federal oversight.[23]

A survey in April 2002 reported that about four hundred thousand embryos are stored in the United States in assisted reproduction clinics. The majority, about 88 percent, were being held in storage by patients who said they hoped to use the embryos at a later time to create a child. (The remainder, it was thought, would fail to develop after thawing, be donated to others, be destroyed by their owners, or be donated to research.) Only 2.8 percent were reported as available for stem cell research.[24]

The Hastings Center, a bioethics think tank in New York, issued a report on embryo use in America in August 2003. The report called for the government to do away with the 2001 policy and establish a regulatory body to oversee all human embryonic research—not just proposals from researchers seeking federal funding for their work—so that important decisions about embryo use are not left to a free-market system.[25]

The Hastings Center report states:

> We cannot have responsible oversight of reprogenetics research and practice, nor of embryo research generally, if we do not first acknowledge that we already support those activities in a wide variety of ways. Our country has already embarked on "one big embryo experiment." If we do not forthrightly accept that first by allowing the federal government to oversee research and practice involving embryos, then the market will be the only mechanism that will distinguish between the acceptable and unacceptable purpose of those activities.[26]

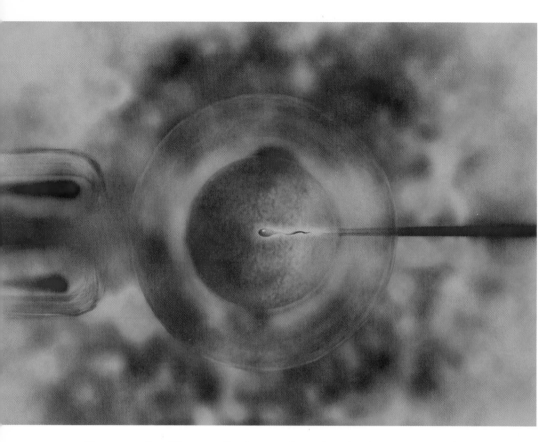

Many people object to the destruction of embryos created during in vitro fertilization. Shown is a computer simulation of the in vitro process.

Concerned about the lack of federal guidelines, the National Academies organized a committee to recommend guidelines researchers should follow when proposing and conducting embryonic stem cell research. The guidelines, unveiled in April 2005, call for a national review of policy on the matter, and it recommends that all institutions conducting such research establish oversight committees. The guidelines also urge that some types of experiments should be out of bounds—experiments, for example, that involve inserting human embryonic stem cells into a human embryo, which would be genetically engineering an embryo, or putting those cells into apes and monkeys. Limits are also placed on some types of work that would put human embryonic stem cells into animals, for fear that human cells would become part of an animal's sex cells or "contribute in a 'major, organized way'" to its brain.[27]

The National Academies' guidelines are not mandatory, but most scientists welcome the guidance.

Critical Point in History

Should the United States reconsider its stance on the use of human embryos in research? Should President Bush hold firm to his decision?

Some ethicists believe that today is a critical point in history. Decisions made in state legislatures and in Congress will have a profound effect on society and medical research in the coming decades. The citizens of California in 2004 voted to invest $3 billion in human embryonic stem cell research. Many newspapers reported that this move might very well turn California into a global center for human embryonic stem cell research.

Even if you are not eligible to vote today, one day you will be. As you now know, the debate over human embryonic stem cell research is complex and filled with many different perspectives, all of which should be respectfully considered in a democratic society.

You may soon find yourself in a similar position to the citizens of California. You may be asked to vote "yes" or "no" on ballot proposals in your state to fund human embryonic stem cell research—or to ban it. Understanding what scientists and policy makers are proposing, and knowing all arguments for and against, will help you make an informed and intelligent decision.

Chapter Notes

Chapter 1 Small Matters of Immense Importance

1. Christopher Reeve, *Still Me* (New York: Random House, 1998), p. 28.

2. "Ron Reagan's remarks at the Democratic convention," *USA Today,* July 29, 2004, <http://www.usatoday.com/news/politicselections/ nation/president/2004-07-29-reagan-speech-text_x.htm> (March 25, 2005).

3. "Catholic Official Says Campaign for Embryonic Stem Cell Research Ignores Ethical and Practical Problems," *United States Conference of Catholic Bishops,* September 30, 2004, <http:// www.usccb.org/comm/archives/2004/04-187.htm> (March 31, 2005).

4. "Recent Developments in Stem Cell Research and Therapy," *Monitoring Stem Cell Research,* a report by The President's Council on Bioethics (Washington, D.C.: January 2004), pp. 127–128.

5. "What are the similarities and differences between embryonic and adult stem cells?" *Stem Cell Information: Stem Cell Basics,* June 10, 2004, <http://stem.cells.nih.gov/info/basics/basics4asp> (August 5, 2004).

6. Ibid.

7. "Recent Developments in Stem Cell Research and Therapy," pp. 123–124.

8. H. M. Blau, T. R. Brazelton, and J. M. Weimann, "The evolving concept of a stem cell: entity or function?" *Cell,* June 29, 2001, pp. 829–841.

9. The National Academy of Sciences, *Stem Cells and the Future of Regenerative Medicine* (Washington, D.C.: National Academy Press, 2002), pp. 19, 23.

10. D. Orlic et al., "Bone Marrow Cells Regenerate Infarcted Myocardium," *Nature,* vol. 410, April 5, 2001, pp. 701–705.

11. Ronda Wendler, "Will Stem Cells Restore Life to Failing Hearts?" *Updates from the Heart,* Texas Heart Institute at St. Luke's Hospital,

April 2004, <http://www.texasheartinstitute.org/AboutUs/News/ articles.cfm#CP_JUMP_7067> (January 28, 2006).

12. The National Academy of Sciences, p. 23.

13. "Nobel Laureates' Letter to President Bush," *WashingtonPost.com*, February 22, 2001, <http://www.washingtonpost.com/ac2/ wp-dyn?pagename=article&node=&contentId=A37117-2001Feb21&notFound=true> (February 16, 2005).

14. Terry Devitt, "Five years later, stem cells still tantalize," *Embryonic Stem Cells: Research at the University of Wisconsin-Madison*, November 4, 2003, <http://www.news.wisc.edu/packages/ stemcells/retro.html> (November 15, 2004).

15. David M. Gilbert, "The future of human embryonic stem cell research: Addressing ethical conflict with responsible scientific research," *Medical Science Monitor*, May 1, 2004, p. RA100.

16. David Hoffman, et al., "Cryopreserved embryos in the United States and their availability for research," *Fertility and Sterility*, May 2003, p. 1063.

17. Claudia Kalb, Debra Rosenberg, et al., "Stem Cell Division," *Newsweek*, October 25, 2004, p. 43.

18. "Human Stem Cells and the Treatment of Disease," *Monitoring Stem Cell Research*, a report by The President's Council on Bioethics (Washington, D.C.: January 2004), pp. 131–140.

19. W. M. Rideout III, et al., "Correction of a genetic defect by nuclear transplantation and combined cell and gene therapy," *Cell*, April 5, 2002, pp. 17–27.

20. William Hurlbut, speaking at "Stem Cells: Science, Ethics and Politics at the Crossroads. Part 2: The Ethics," a symposium at The Salk Institute, October 2, 2004, <http://www.ucsd.tv/library-test. asp?showID=9064> (March 16, 2005).

21. "Current Federal Law and Policy," *Monitoring Stem Cell Research*, a report by The President's Council on Bioethics (Washington, D.C.: January 2004), pp. 28–29.

22. "Remarks by the President on Stem Cell Research," *The White House*, August 9, 2001, <http://www.whitehouse.gov/news/releases/ 2001/08/20010809-2.html > (March 16, 2005).

23. George Daley, "Missed Opportunities in Embryonic Stem-Cell Research," *New England Journal of Medicine*, August 12, 2004, pp. 627–628.

24. "Human Embryonic Stem Cells Express an Immunogenic Non-human Sialic Acid," *Nature Medicine*, February 2005, pp. 228–232.

25. "Fact Sheet: Embryonic Stem Cell Research," United States Department of Health and Human Services, July 14, 2004, <http://www.os.hhs.gov/news/press/2004pres/20040714b.html> (March 16, 2005).

26. Heather Timmons, "Britain Grants License to Make Human Embryos for Stem Cells," *The New York Times*, August 12, 2004, p. A4.

27. Constance Holden, "U.K. Gives Cloning OK," *Science*, August 20, 2004, p. 1102.

28. Associated Press, "Britain Grants 'Dolly' Scientist Cloning License," *The New York Times*, February 9, 2005, p. A6.

Chapter 2   Adult Stem Cell Research

1. National Institutes of Health, *Stem Cells: Scientific Progress and Future Research Directions* (Washington, D.C.: June 2001), p. 23.

2. Ibid., p. 25.

3. The National Academy of Sciences, *Stem Cells and the Future of Regenerative Medicine* (Washington, D.C.: National Academy Press, 2002), p. 24.

4. Gareth Cook, "From adult stem cells comes debate," *The Boston Globe*, November 1, 2004, <http://www.boston.com/yourlife/health/diseases/articles/2004/11/01/from_adult_stem_cells_comes_debate/> (January 28, 2006).

5. The Yomiuri Shimbun, "Japanese doctors claim heart disease breakthrough," *TimesLeader.com*, August 27, 2005, <http://www.timesleader.com/mld/timesleader/news/world/12494617.htm> (January 28, 2006).

6. "Stem Cells Improve Heart Function of Seriously Ill Heart Failure Patients," *American Heart Association*, April 22, 2003, <http://

www.americanheart.org/presenter.jhtml?identifier=3011068>
(August 31, 2005).

7. Nicholas Wade, "The Uncertain Science of Growing Heart Cells,"
   The New York Times, March 14, 2005, p. A-1.

8. Ronda Wendler, "Will Stem Cells Restore Life to Failing Hearts,"
   Updates from the Heart, Texas Heart Institute at St. Luke's
   Episcopal Hospital, April 2004, <http://www.texasheartinstitute.
   org/AboutUs/News/articles.cfm#CP_JUMP_7067> (January 28,
   2006).

9. "Clinical Trial for Stem Cell Therapy Reaches Major Milestone,"
   Texas Heart Institute at St. Luke's Episcopal Hospital, July 21, 2005,
   <http://www.texasheartinstitute.org/AboutUs/News/
   archive.cfm> (January 28, 2006).

10. Wade, p. A-1.

11. Ibid.

12. Ibid.

13. Ibid.

14. "History of Marrow and Blood Cell Transplants," *National Marrow
    Donor Program*, October 5, 2004, <http://www.marrow.org/
    NMDP/history_of_transplants.html> (December 13, 2004).

15. "Transplant Biology and Therapy: Historical Overview," *University
    of Minnesota Cancer Center*, August 16, 2001, <http://www.cancer.
    umn.edu/page/research/trsplant/bmthist.html> (December 14,
    2004).

16. National Institutes of Health, p. 46.

17. "History of Marrow and Blood Cell Transplants."

18. National Institutes of Health, p. 33.

19. The National Academy of Sciences, pp. 19–21.

20. "What is known about adult stem cell differentiation?" *Stem Cell
    Information: Stem Cell Basics*, June 10, 2004, <http://
    stemcells.nih.gov/info/basics/basics4.asp> (March 21, 2005).

21. Suzanne Kadereit, "Adult Stem Cells," *International Society for Stem
    Cell Research*, February 2, 2005, <http://www.isscr.org/public/
    adultstemcells.htm> (March 22, 2005).

22. David Prentice, "Adult Stem Cells," in Appendix K of *Monitoring Stem Cell Research*, a report by The President's Council on Bioethics (Washington, D.C.: January 2004), p. 315.

23. The National Academy of Sciences, p. 23.

24. Ibid., p. 21.

25. National Institutes of Health, p. 44.

26. Prentice, pp. 314–319.

27. Kadereit.

28. A. Otani, et al., "Bone Marrow Derived Stem Cells Target Retinal Astrocytes and Can Promote or Inhibit Retinal Angiogenesis," *Nature Medicine*, September 2002, vol. 8, pp. 1004–1010.

29. R. Poulson, et al., "Bone Marrow Stem Cells Contribute to Healing of the Kidney," *Journal of the American Society of Nephrology*, vol. 14, 2004, pp. S48–S54.

30. E. Lagasse, et al., "Purified Hematopoietic Stem Cells Can Differentiate Into Hepatocytes in Vivo," *Nature Medicine*, vol. 6, November 2000, pp. 1229–1234.

31. Prentice, p. 316.

32. Diedtra Henderson, "Stem cells target tumors in mice: Guided missiles deliver drug to cancer site," *The* (Newark, N.J.) *Star-Ledger*, November 3, 2004, p. 8.

33. Robert Lanza and Nadia Rosenthal, "The Stem Cell Challenge," *Scientific American*, June 2004, p. 99.

34. The National Academy of Sciences, p. 29.

35. Y. Jiang, et al., "Pluripotency of mesenchymal stem cells derived from adult marrow," *Nature,* July 4, 2002, pp. 41–49.

36. Y. Jiang, et al., "Multipotent progenitor cells can be isolated from postnatal murine bone marrow, muscle, and brain," *Experimental Hematology*, August 30, 2002, pp. 896–904.

37. Cook.

38. "The Potential of Adult Stem Cell Research," *Stem Cell Information: NIH Fact Sheet on Human Pluripotent Stem Cell Research Guidelines*, July 19, 2004, <http://stemcells.nih.gov/news/newsArchives/stemfactsheet.asp> (March 22, 2005).

39. The National Academy of Sciences, p. 26.

40. Karl Sylvester and Michael Longaker, "Stem Cells: Review and Update," *Archives of Surgery*, January 2004, p. 96.

41. "Adult Stem Cells from Other Sources," *Monitoring Stem Cell Research*, a report by the President's Council on Bioethics (Washington, D.C.: January 2004), p. 126.

42. Prentice, p. 312.

43. Neil D. Theise, "Stem Cell Research: Elephants in the Room," *Mayo Clinic Proceedings*, vol. 78, 2003, p. 1005.

Chapter 3 Human Embryonic Stem Cell Research

1. Richard Lacayo, "How Bush Got There," *Time*, August 20, 2001, p. 20.

2. Staff of the President's Council on Bioethics, "Notes on Early Human Development," in Appendix A of *Monitoring Stem Cell Research*, a report by The President's Council on Bioethics (Washington, D.C.: January 2004), pp. 173–176.

3. Terry Devitt, "Wisconsin scientists culture elusive embryonic stem cells," *Embryonic Stem Cells: Research at the University of Wisconsin-Madison*, November 5, 1998, <http://www.news.wisc.edu/packages/stemcells/3327.html> (January 12, 2005).

4. John Gearhart, "New Potential for Human Embryonic Stem Cells," *Science*, November 6, 1998, pp. 1061–1062.

5. "Stem Cell Basics: What are embryonic stem cells?" *Stem Cell Information*, June 11, 2004, <http://stemcells.nih.gov/info/basics/basics3.asp> (August 5, 2004).

6. "NIH Awards a National Stem Cell Bank and New Centers of Excellence in Translational Human Stem Cell Research," *NIH News*, October 3, 2005, <http://www.nih.gov/news/pr/oct2005/od-03.htm> (April 20, 2006).

7. "Human ES Cell (hESC) Lines," *International Society for Stem Cell Research*, January 5, 2005, <http://www.isscr.org/science/sclines.htm> (January 12, 2005).

8. Claudia Kalb, "Welcome to the Stem Cell States," *Newsweek*, December 6, 2004, p. 54.

9. Alvin Powell, "From the laboratory to the patient: Stem Cell Institute will call on expertise from around University to turn research into therapy," *The Harvard Gazette*, April 22, 2004, <http://www.news.harvard.edu/gazette/2004/04.22/99-StemOver.html> (January 14, 2005).

10. Ibid.

11. Gareth Cook, "Harvard Provost OKs Procedure," *The Boston Globe*, March 20, 2005, p. A-29.

12. National Institutes of Health, *Stem Cells: Scientific Progress and Future Research Directions* (Washington, D.C.: June 2001), p. ES-9.

13. James A. Thomson, et al., "Embryonic Stem Cell Lines Derived from Human Blastocysts," *Science*, November 6, 1998, pp. 1145–1147.

14. "Stem Cell Basics: What are embryonic stem cells?"

15. Anthony L. Komaroff and George Q. Daley, "Harnessing Stem Cells," *Newsweek*, December 6, 2004, p. 54.

16. Gina Kolata, "Stem Cell Science Gets Limelight; Now it Needs a Cure," *The New York Times*, August 24, 2004, p. F1.

17. "Promise of Stem Cells Amplified; New Evidence Shows Cells May Help Treat Many Disorders Including Paralysis and Brain Cancer," *Society for Neuroscience*, n.d., <http://web.sfn.org/content/AboutSfN1/NewsReleases/am2004_human.html> (January 7, 2005).

18. Hans Keirstead, G. Nistor, G. Bernal, M Totiu, F. Cloutier, K. Sharp, and O. Steward, "Human embryonic stem cell-derived oligodendrocyte progenitor cell transplants remyelinate and restore locomotion after spinal cord injury," *Journal of Neuroscience*, vol. 19, May 11, 2005, pp. 4694–4705.

19. Paul Elias, Associated Press, "Stem cell researcher makes paralyzed rats walk," *SFGate.com,* December 17, 2004, <http://www.sfgate.com/cgi-bin/article.cgi?file=/news/archive/2004/12/17/financial1423EST0176.DTL> (January 31, 2005).

20. "Spinal Cord Injury," *Neurosurgery Today.org,* American Association of Neurological Surgeons, November 2005, <http://www.neurosurgery.org/what/patient_e/spinal.asp> (January 31, 2006).

21. Andrew Pollack, "Moving Stem Cells Front and Center," *The New York Times*, February 23, 2005, p. C-1.

22. "National Diabetes Fact Sheet," *Centers for Disease Control and Prevention*, January 31, 2006, <http://www.cdc.gov/diabetes/pubs/estimates.htm#prev> (January 31, 2006).

23. "Type 1 Diabetes," *American Diabetes Association,* n.d., <http://www.diabetes.org/type-1-diabetes.jsp> (January 23, 2005).

24. Maya Pines, "Are Stem Cells the Answer?" *Howard Hughes Medical Institute Bulletin*, March 2002, pp. 10–17.

25. "A Family Fighting for a Cure," *Juvenile Diabetes Research Foundation International,* April 28, 2003, <http://www.jdrf.org/index.cfm?page_id=100172> (January 22, 2005).

26. Y. Hori, et al., "Growth inhibitors promote differentiation of insulin-producing tissue from embryonic stem cells," *Proceedings of the National Academy of Sciences*, vol. 99, December 2002, pp. 16105–16110.

27. "Global Conference Highlights Stem Cells' Role as Models for Disease Study and Treatment," *Juvenile Diabetes Research Foundation*, July 28, 2004, <http://www.jdrf.org/index.cfm?page_id=102800> (January 23, 2005).

28. Y. Dor, J. Brown, O. I. Martinez, and D. A. Melton, "Adult pancreatic beta-cells are formed by self-duplication rather than stem-cell differentiation," *Nature*, vol. 429, May 6, 2004, pp. 41–46.

29. "Insulin-Producing Pancreatic Cells Are Replenished by Duplication," *Howard Hughes Medical Institute*, May 5, 2004, <http://hhmi.org/news/melton5.html> (January 23, 2005).

30. Rick Weiss, "Two Studies Bolster Stem Cells' Use in Fighting Disease," *The Washington Post*, September 27, 2004, p. A3.

31. Ibid.

32. Jim Giles, "Stem cells home in on brain cancer," *News@Nature.com*, October 25, 2004, <http://www.nature.com/news/2004/041025/pf/041025-6_pf.html> (January 23, 2005).

33. Ibid.

34. "An Introduction to Clinical Trials," *Clinical Trials.gov: A Service of the National Institutes of Health*, January 13, 2005, <http://www.clinicaltrials.gov/ct/info/whatis#whatis> (January 24, 2005).

35. "Information on Clinical Trials and Human Research Studies," *Clinical Trials.gov: A Service of the National Institutes of Health*, n.d., <http://www.clinicaltrials.gov/ct/search> (January 18, 2005).

36. "Clinical application still years away," *Embryonic Stem Cells: Research at the University of Wisconsin-Madison*, n.d., <http://www.news.wisc.edu/packages/stemcells/patients.html> (January 25, 2005).

37. "Panel: Clinical use of embryonic stem cells jeopardized by policy on federal funding," *Johns Hopkins Medicine*, November 10, 2003, <http://www.hopkinsmedicine.org/Press_releases/2003/11_10_03.html> (January 25, 2005).

38. Maria J. Martin, Alysson Muotri, Fred Gage, and Ajit Varki, "Human embryonic stem cells express an immunogenic nonhuman sialic acid," *Nature Medicine: Advance Online Publication*, January 24, 2004, <http://www.nature.com/nm/journal/vaop/ncurrent/pdf/nm1181.pdf> (January 24, 2004).

39. "Stem Cell Basics: What are the potential uses of human stem cells and the obstacles that must be overcome before these potential uses will be realized?" *Stem Cell Information*, June 10, 2004, <http://stemcells.nih.gov/info/basics/basics6.asp> (January 18, 2004).

Chapter 4 Nuclear Transfer

1. "Cloning: Present Uses and Promises," *National Institutes of Health: Office of Science Policy and Planning*, April 27, 1998, <http://ospp.od.nih.gov/policy/cloning.asp> (February 7, 2005).

2. "Somatic Cell Nuclear Transfer (Therapeutic Cloning)," *Association of American Medical Colleges*, n.d., <http://www.aamc.org/advocacy/library/research/res0003.htm> (January 28, 2005).

3. "Cloning: Present Uses and Promises."

4. "Briefing Notes on Dolly," *Roslin Institute,* n.d., <http://www.roslin.ac.uk/public/12-12-97-bn.html> (September 16, 2005).

5. Ibid.

6. Michael D. Lemonick, et al., "Woof, Woof! Who's Next?" *Time*, August 15, 2005, p. 54.

7. Richard Mollard, "Reproductive Cloning," *International Society for Stem Cell Research*, n.d., <http://www.isscr.org/public/reproductive.htm> (February 2, 2005).

8. Mary V. Wright, "Cloning: A Select Chronology, 1997–2003," *CRS Report for Congress* (Washington, D.C.: The Library of Congress: Congressional Research Service, August 19, 2003), p. CRS-3, <http://www.fas.org/spp/civil/crs/RL31211.pdf>.

9. Mollard.

10. "Statement on Human Cloning," *The Interacademy Panel*, September 22, 2003, <http://www4.nationalacademies.org/iap/IAPHome.nsf/weblinks/WWWW-5RHG35/$file/Cloning_Stat_EN.pdf?OpenElement> (September 16, 2005).

11. "IAP confirms its support for therapeutic cloning," *The InterAcademy Panel on International Issues*, n.d., <http://www4.nationalacademies.org/iap/iaphome.nsf/weblinks/WWWW-5RHFLT?OpenDocument> (February 7, 2005).

12. W.M. Rideout III, K. Hochedlinger, M. Kyba, G.Q. Daley, and R. Jaenisch, "Correction of a genetic defect by nuclear transplantation and combined cell and gene therapy," *Cell*, April 5, 2002, pp. 17–27.

13. David Cameron, "Life, death and stem cells," *Whitehead Institute for Biomedical Research*, November 10, 2004, <http://www.wi.mit.edu/news/archives/2004/cpa_1110.html> (February 10, 2005).

14. "Cloning: Present Uses and Promises."

15. Rudolf Jaenisch, "The Biology of Nuclear Cloning and the Potential of Embryonic Stem Cells for Transplantation Therapy," in Appendix N of *Monitoring Stem Cell Research*, a report by The President's Council on Bioethics (Washington, D.C.: January 2004), p. 396.

16. Wright, p. CRS-2.

17. "Pig research halt 'a commercial decision,'" *BBC News*, August 14, 2000, <http://news.bbc.co.uk/1/health/879703.stm> (September 17, 2005).

18. Wright, pp. CRS-5 and -6.

19. Constance Holding, "Primate Parthenotes Yield Stem Cells," *Science*, February 1, 2002, pp. 779–780.

20. "Researchers Report First Evidence That Nuclear Transplantation (Therapeutic Cloning) Can Eliminate Tissue Rejection," *Advanced Cell Technology*, June 3, 2002, <http://www.advancedcell.com/press-releases/> (January 31, 2006).

21. Hugh Auchincloss and Joseph V. Bonventre, "Transplanting cloned cells into therapeutic promise," *Nature Biotechnology*, vol. 20, July 2002, pp. 665–666.

22. W. S. Hwang, et al., "Evidence of a Pluripotent Human Embryonic Stem Cell Line Derived from a Cloned Blastocyst," *Science*, March 12, 2004, p. 1669.

23. W. S. Hwang et al., "Patient-specific embryonic stem cells derived from human SCNT blastocysts," *Science,* vol. 308, June 17, 2005, pp. 1777–1783.

24. Seoul National University Investigation Commitee, "Summary of the Final Report on Hwang's Research Allegation," *Seoul National University*, January 10, 2006, <http://snu.ac.kr/engsu> (January 13, 2006).

25. Jennifer Couzin, "Hwang Apologizes for Stem Cell Debate," January 12, 2006, *ScienceNOW Daily News,* <http://sciencenow.sciencemag.org/cgi/content/full/2006/112/1> (January 13, 2006).

26. "Scientists 'cloned human embryos': Stem cells extracted to be used for medical research," *CNN.com*, February 12, 2004, <http://www.cnn.com/2004/HEALTH/02/12/science.clone> (November 16, 2004).

27. The President's Council on Bioethics, *Human Cloning and Human Dignity: An Ethical Inquiry* (Washington, D.C.: July 2002), p. xxx.

28. Jason Hipp and Anthony Atala, "Tissue engineering, stem cells, cloning, and parthenogenesis: New paradigms for therapy," *Journal of Experimental and Clinical Reproduction*, December 8, 2004, <http://www.pubmedcentral.nih.gov/articlerender.fcgi?artid=539246> (February 11, 2005).

29. Ibid.

30. Jose B. Cibelli, Robert P. Lanza, and Michael D. West, with Carol Ezzell, "The First Human Cloned Embryo," *Scientific American*, November 24, 2001, <http://www.sciam.com/ article.c fm?articleID=0008B8F9-AC62-1C75-9381809EC588EF21> (February 8, 2005).

31. Andrew Pollack, "Scientists Seek Ways to Rebuild the Body, Bypassing Embryos," *The New York Times*, December 18, 2001, p. F-6.

32. Minutes of the 19th Meeting of The President's Council on Bioethics, held Friday, December 3, 2004, in Washington, D.C., <http://www.bioethics.gov/transcripts/dec04/session6.html> (February 12, 2005).

33. Ibid.

34. Ibid.

35. Testimony by George Q. Daley to the Senate Appropriations Subcommittee on Labor, Health and Human Services, Education, Hearing on "An Alternative Method for Obtaining Embryonic Stem Cells," Washington, D.C., July 12, 2005, <http:// www.isscr.org/public/testimony_daley.htm> (September 19, 2005).

36. Douglas A. Melton, George Q. Daley, and Charles G. Jennings, "Altered Nuclear Transfer in Stem Cell Research—A Flawed Proposal," *New England Journal of Medicine*, vol. 351, no. 27, December 30, 2004, pp. 2790–2791.

Chapter 5 Public Policy

1. Frederic Golden, "Stem Winder," *CNN/TIME—America's Best*, 2001, <http://www.cnn.com/SPECIALS/2001/americasbest/ science.medicine/pro.jthomson.html> (January 14, 2005).

2. Ibid.

3. Andrew Pollack, "Measure Passed, California Weighs Its Future as a Stem Cell Epicenter," *The New York Times*, November 4, 2004, p. C-10.

4. "Key Facts Points About Prop 71," *Yes on 71: California Stem Cell Research and Cures Initiative*, n.d., <http://www.yeson71.com/ fact_sheets.php> (March 9, 2005).

5. Ibid.

6. Fionna Hutton, "Governor Arnold Schwarzenegger Endorses Prop 71," *Yes on 71: California Stem Cell Research and Cures Initiative,* October 18, 2004, <http://www.yeson71.com/ news_rel_1018.php> (February 3, 2006).

7. Kathryn Jean Lopez, "Braveheart Stands Athwart a Brave New World," *National Review Online,* November 1, 2004, <http:// www.nationalreview.com/interrogatory/gibson200411010950.asp> (March 11, 2005).

8. Pollack.

9. Tom Vincz, Director of Communications for the New Jersey Department of the Treasury, personal communication with author, April 25, 2006.

10. "Codey: This Moment in History Has Given Us the Opportunity to Chart a New Course," *Office of the Acting Governor,* January 11, 2005, <http://www.state.nj.us/cgi-bin/governor/njnewsline/ view_article.pl?id=2315> (March 13, 2005).

11. Terry Devitt, "Wisconsin posed to invest $750 million in biomedical research," *Embryonic Stem Cell Research at the University of Wisconsin-Madison,* November 20, 2004, <http:// www.news.wisc.edu/packages/stemcells/10446.html> (January 18, 2005).

12. Associated Press, "Massachusetts allows work on embryo stem cells," *The* (New Jersey) *Star-Ledger,* June 1, 2005, p.8.

13. Dennis Cauchon, "Divisive issues on state agendas: Use of stem cells is one of many," *USA Today,* December 15, 2004, p. A3.

14. "National Institutes of Health," *National Institutes of Health,* May 17, 2004, <http://www.nih.gov/about/NIHoverview.html> (March 9, 2005).

15. Judith A. Johnson and Erin Williams, "Stem Cell Research," *CRS Report for Congress* (Washington, D.C.: The Library of Congress: Congressional Research Service, August 13, 2004), p. CRS-3, <http://www.fas.org/spp/civil/crs/RL31015.pdf>.

16. Ibid., p. CRS-4.

17. Ibid.

18. Ibid., pp. CRS-4 and CRS-5.

19. "President Discusses Stem Cell Research," *The White House*, August 9, 2001, <http://www.whitehouse.gov/news/releases/2001/08/20010809-2.html> (March 16, 2005).

20. Tommy G. Thompson, "Why Bush's stem-cell policy is reasoned— and why it's working," *USA Today*, August 18, 2004, p. 11A.

21. Kyla Dunn, "The Politics of Stem Cells," *NOVA*, April 2005, <http://www.pbs.org/wgbh/nova/sciencenow/dispatches/050413.html> (February 3, 2006).

22. Letter from the American Association for the Advancement of Science Chief Executive Officer Alan Leshner, July 18, 2005, <http://aaas.org> (September 19, 2005).

23. Jim Hopkins, "Stem cell's promise pits jobs vs. values," *USATODAY.com*, February 15, 2005, <http://www.usatoday.com/news/health/2005-02-15-stem-cell-usat_x.htm> (March 3, 2005).

24. Kim Tai-gyu, "World Stem Cell Hub Opens in Seoul," October 19, 2005, <http://search.hankooki.com/times/times_view.php?term=world+stem+cell+hub++&path=hankooki3/times/lpage/200510/kt2005101917235910440.htm&media=kt> (February 9, 2006).

25. Debora Spar, "The Business of Stem Cells," *New England Journal of Medicine*, July 15, 2004, p. 211.

26. Elisabeth Rosenthal, "Britain Embraces Stem Cell Research," *The New York Times*, August 24, 2004, p. F-6.

27. Heather Timmons, "Britain Grants License to Make Human Embryos for Stem Cells," August 12, 2004, *The New York Times*, p. A-4.

28. "Fact Sheet: Embryonic Stem Cell Research," *U.S. Department of Health and Human Services*, August 18, 2004, <http://www.hhs.gov/news/press/2004pres/20040714b.html> (March 10, 2005).

29. "General Assembly approves declaration banning all forms of cloning," *United Nations News Centre*, March 9, 2005, <http://www.un.org/apps/news/story.asp?NewsID=13576&Cr=cloning&Crl=> (March 10, 2005).

30. "UN vote urges human cloning ban," *BBC News*, March 8, 2005, <http://bbc.co.uk/2/hi/health/4328919.stm> (March 9, 2005).

31. Spar, pp. 211–213.

32. Ibid.

33. Sei Chong and Dennis Normile, with reporting by Gretchen Vogel, "How Young Korean Researchers Helped Unearth a Scandal," *Science*, January 6, 2006, p. 22.

34. Dennis Normile, Gretchen Vogel, and Jennifer Couzin, "South Korean Team's Remaining Human Stem Cell Claim Demolished," *Science*, January 13, 2006, p. 157.

35. Seoul National University Investigation Committee, "Summary of the Final Report on Hwang's Research Allegation," *Seoul National University*, January 10, 2006, <http://www.snu.ac.kr/> (January 13, 2006).

36. "Fact Sheet: Embryonic Stem Cell Research."

37. Ibid.

Chapter 6   The Concerns

1. John H. Evans, "Cloning Adam's Rib: A Primer on Religious Responses to Cloning," a report prepared for the Pew Forum on Religion and Public Life, n.d., available at <http://pewforum.org/publications/reports/adamsrib.pdf> (March 1, 2005).

2. Cynthia B. Cohen, "Open Possibilities, Close Concerns: The import of religious views on the future of stem cell research," *The Park Ridge Center for Health, Faith, and Ethics*, January/February 2000, <http://www.parkridgecenter.org/Page35.html> (March 4, 2005).

3. Ibid.

4. Tim Kershner, "Synod OKs federally funded stem cell research," *United Church News, Online Edition*, 2001, <http://www.ucc.org/ucnews/gsa01/stem.htm> (September 20, 2005).

5. Courtney S. Campbell, "Cloning Human Beings: Religious Perspectives on Human Cloning," a commissioned paper in *Cloning Human Beings*, a report by the National Bioethics Advisory Committee (Rockville, Md.: June 1997), pp. 22–25, <http://www.

georgetown.edu/research/nrcbl/nbac/pubs.html> (February 25, 2005).

6. "Donum Vitae (Instruction on Respect for Human Life in its Origin and on the Dignity of Procreation: Replies to Certain Questions of the Day)," *The Roman Curia: Congregation for the Doctrine of Faith*, February 22, 1987, <http://www.vatican.va/roman_curia/congregations/cfaith/documents/rc_con_cfaith_doc_19870222_respect-for-human-life_en.html> (March 1, 2005).

7. Pope John Paul II, "To the President of the United States of America, H.E. George Walker Bush," *The Roman Curia: The Holy Father*, July 23, 2001, <http://www.vatican.va/holy_father/john_paul_ii/speeches/2001/documents/hf_jp-ii_spe_20010723_president-bush_en.html> (March 1, 2005).

8. Aline H. Kalbian, "Stem Cells and the Catholic Church," *The Stem Cell Controversy: Debating the Issues*, edited by Michael Ruse and Christopher A. Pynes (Amherst, N.Y.: Prometheus Books, 2003), pp. 183–184.

9. Pontifical Academy for Life, "Declaration on the Production and the Scientific and Therapeutic Use of Human Embryonic Stem Cells," August 25, 2000, <http://www.vatican.va/roman_curia/pontifical_academies/acdlife/documents/rc_pa_acdlife_doc_20000824_cellule-staminali_en.html> (February 24, 2005).

10. Ibid.

11. "Testimony of Margaret Farley, Yale University," *Ethical Issues in Human Stem Cell Research*, a report by the National Bioethics Advisory Commission (Rockville, Md.: September 1999), pp. D1–D4, <http://www.georgetown.edu/research/nrcbl/nbac/pubs.html> (February 25, 2005).

12. Nicholas Wade, "Embryo Cell Research: A Clash of Values," *The New York Times*, July 2, 1999, p. A13.

13. Elliot N. Dorff, "Stem Cell Research," *Committee on Jewish Law and Standards of the Rabbinical Assembly*, March 13, 2002, <http://www.rabbinicalassembly.org/teshuvot/docs/19912000/dorff_stemcell.pdf > (March 4, 2005).

14. Pauline Dubkin Yearwood, "Jewish Views on Stem Cell Research," *My Jewish Learning.com*, n.d., <http://www.myjewishlearning. com/ideas_belief/bioethics/Overview_Genetic_Issues/Gene_ Therapy_And_Genetic_Engineering/Bioethics_StemCell_CJN. htm> (February 28, 2005).

15. "Resolution in Support of Research and Stem Cell Education," *The Rabbinical Assembly*, April 2003, <http://www. rabbinicalassembly.org/docs/2003resolutions2.pdf> (February 28, 2005).

16. Dorff.

17. Paul Lauritzen, "Report on the Ethics of Stem Cell Research," in Appendix G of *Monitoring Stem Cell Research*, a report by The President's Council on Bioethics (Washington, D.C.: January 2004), pp. 248–249.

18. "Orthodox Union's position re: Stem Cell Research," *Jewish Law: Law and Policy*, July 26, 2001, <http://www.jlaw.com/LawPolicy/ stemcellou.html> (February 28, 2005).

19. Cynthia B. Cohen, "Open Possibilities, Close Concerns: The import of religious views on the future of stem cell research," *The Park Ridge Center for Health, Faith, and Ethics*, January/February 2000, <http://www.parkridgecenter.org/Page35.html> (March 4, 2005).

20. "Recent Developments in the Ethical and Policy Debates," *Monitoring Stem Cell Research*, a report by the President's Council on Bioethics (Washington, D.C.: January 2004), pp. 54–57.

21. "Ron Reagan's Remarks at the Democratic Convention," *USA Today*, July 29, 2004, <http://www.usatoday.com/news/ politicselections/nation/president/2004-07-29-reagan-speech- text_x.htm> (March 25, 2005).

22. Ronald M. Green, "The Stem Cell Conundrum," *Religion in the News*, Fall 2001, <http://www.trincoll.edu/depts/csrpl/ RINVol3No3/RINVol4No3/stem%20cell.htm> (March 1, 2005).

23. Eric Trump, "Stem Cell Divisions," *Bioethics Research at the Hastings Center*, October 18, 2004, <http://www.thehastingscenter. org/news/features/scdivisions.asp> (March 4, 2005).

24. David I. Hoffman, et al., "Cryopreserved embryos in the United States and their availability for research," *Fertility and Sterility*, May 2003, p. 1063.

25. Trump.

26. Erik Parens and Lori P. Knowles, "Reprogenetics and Public Policy: Reflections and Recommendations," July/August 2003, *Hastings Center Report*, p. S-18, <http://www.thehastingscenter.org/ publications/reports.asp> (March 6, 2005).

27. "Guidelines Released for Embryonic Stem Cell Research," *The National Academies*, April 26, 2005, <http://www4. nationalacademies.org/news.nsf/isbn/0309096537?OpenDocument> (September 18, 2005).

Glossary

adult stem cells—Stem cells found in the blood, tissue, and organs of mature organisms, such as children and adults, as well as in the after-products of birth, such as the umbilical cord blood and placenta. These undifferentiated cells can generate specialized cells that are the same as those in which the adult stem cell resides.

Alzheimer's disease—A disease of the brain, usually in older people, that causes a gradual and steady loss of memory and mental abilities.

amplify—In science, to increase a sample size or cell population.

artifact—See **biological artifact**.

bioethics—The study of how important decisions and developments in the biological sciences affect the well-being of a society.

biological artifact—A cell mass, created by inserting genetic material into an enucleated egg, that cannot develop beyond the basic embryolike cellular system because the inserted DNA is modified to prevent embryogenesis.

biotechnology—The application of technology to the fields of biological science.

blastocyst—The developmental stage four to five days after the egg has been fertilized, which resembles a hollow, fluid-filled ball made up of about one hundred fifty cells. The outer cells are called the trophoblast, and the inner cells are called the inner cell mass.

bone marrow—The soft tissue in the inner cavity of bones that contains a mixture of different cell types. This mixture includes stem cells known to generate all of the body's blood cells as well as bone, cartilage, and fat cells.

cell-based therapies—Treatments intended to cure disease by introducing cells into a patient. These can be stem cells, stem cell-derived specialized cells, or cells extracted from dead fetuses. Also called regenerative medicine.

chemotherapy—The use of chemicals to treat or control disease.

clinical trial—A study in which a new treatment for a disease is tested in patients to ensure that the treatment works and is safe.

clone—An organism genetically identical to another organism.

culture (verb)—To grow cells in a laboratory setting, usually in a culture dish in a nutrient solution called culture medium.

differentiate—The process of specialization of a stem cell or progenitor cell into a cell of specific function, such as a liver cell or a muscle cell.

DNA (deoxyribonucleic acid)—The genetic material of an organism.

egg cell—The female reproductive cell.

embryo—In humans, a developing egg cell from the time it is fertilized (or stimulated to grow), up to the eighth week of development, at which point an embryo is called a fetus.

embryonic stem cells—Stem cells derived from the inner cell mass of a blastocyst. These stem cells are pluripotent, meaning they can generate many different types of specialized cells.

fallopian tube—A tube in the female reproductive system through which an egg from the ovary is directed toward the uterus.

fetus—A growing human embryo from the eighth week of pregnancy to birth.

genome—The genetic material of an organism.

germ layers—The three different layers of cells (mesoderm, endoderm, and ectoderm) that form from the inner cell mass as a blastocyst develops.

hematopoietic stem cells (HSCs)—Stem cells that generate all of the blood cells in the body.

human embryonic germ cells (HEGCs)—Pluripotent stem cells obtained from the tissue of dead fetuses.

immune system—The system in the body that reacts to the introduction of foreign material, such as bacteria, and destroys the invading material.

inner cell mass—Cells that develop inside a zygote after it becomes a blastocyst.

insulin—A hormone secreted by tissue in the pancreas that helps transport glucose into cells in the body.

in vitro—Latin for "in glass"; an artificial environment, such as a culture dish or test.

medical therapy—Any type of treatment, such as a procedure or a drug, given to patients to cure disease or provide relief from the symptoms of a disease.

mesenchymal stem cells (MSCs)—Stem cells that are mainly found in bone marrow that can generate many tissue types, such as muscle, cartilage, bone, fat, and connective tissue.

multipotent adult progenitor cell (MAPC)—A possible new type of cell discovered by University of Wisconsin researchers that has been shown in some studies to be pluripotent, or capable of creating many different cell types.

neuron—A type of brain cell that transmits nerve impulses.

nuclear transfer—A scientific technique in which the nuclear material of one cell is transferred to another cell.

oligodendrocytes—Brain cells that form a substance called myelin. Myelin insulates the "wiring" of neurons that carry nerve impulses.

ovaries—The organs in the female reproductive system that contain the egg cells.

Parkinson's disease—A disease that destroys the nerve cells in the part of the brain that controls movement.

parthenogenesis—A process in which an egg cell is artificially stimulated to grow without the introduction of sperm for fertilization. Parthenogenesis sometimes occurs in nature in insects, lizards, birds, snakes, and fish, but not in mammals.

parthenote—A developing egg cell that is created through parthenogenesis.

petri dish—A small, round plastic or glass dish with a cover in which cells and tissues are placed in culture to grow and propagate.

placenta—The organ that grows in a uterus during a pregnancy to nourish the developing fetus, eliminate waste products, and aid in the exchange of gases.

plastic—Able to make many different types of specialized cells.

pluripotent stem cell—A stem cell that is capable of producing any cell in the human body except for some specific cells that develop to implant and nourish an embryo that is growing inside a uterus.

progenitor cell—The "daughter" cell of a stem cell that can generate more specialized cells. Unlike stem cells, progenitor cells cannot make copies of themselves for self-renewal.

propagate—To increase or multiply.

regenerative medicine—See **cell-based therapies**.

reproductive cloning—The use of nuclear transfer to create a blastocyst to be implanted in a uterus in an attempt to create a "born" organism that is genetically identical to the organism from which the donor DNA was taken.

somatic cell—Any cell in the body except for the sperm and egg cells, which are called germline cells.

somatic cell nuclear transfer (SCNT)—A technique in which the DNA of a somatic cell, or any cell in the body other than an egg or sperm cell, is transferred into an egg cell that has had its own DNA removed. The egg is then stimulated to divide.

sperm cell—The male reproductive cell.

stem cell—An unspecialized cell that can make identical copies of itself through cell division and which can generate many different types of specialized cells.

stem cell line—A population of stem cells that can be grown, and which can self-renew, in a laboratory culture dish over a long period of time.

teratoma—A tumor that is made up of cells from the three different germ layers.

therapeutic cloning—Somatic cell nuclear transfer that is done to create a blastocyst from which embryonic stem cells can be obtained for research and therapeutic purposes.

totipotent cell—A stem cell capable of producing any cell in the human body, including an entire organism. The zygote is totipotent.

trophoblast—Cells that make up the hollow sphere of the blastocyst that help implant the blastocyst into the uterus and form the placenta.

umbilical cord—In mammals, the cord connecting the fetus to the placenta, through which the fetus is nourished. The cord contains arteries and veins that circulate fetal blood stem cells, which after birth can be frozen for potential, later use.

zygote—The egg cell after it has been fertilized by a sperm cell and before division starts. It is called a blastocyst after it has divided many times.

Further Reading

Books

Fridell, Ron. *Decoding Life: Unraveling the Mysteries of the Genome.* New York: Lerner, 2005.

Hyde, Margaret O., and John F. Setaro. *Medicine's Brave New World: Bioengineering and the New Genetics.* Brookfield, Conn.: Twenty-First Century Books, 2001.

Panno, Joseph. *Stem Cell Research: Medical Applications and Ethical Controversy.* New York: Facts on File, 2004.

Parson, Ann B. *The Proteus Effect: Stem Cells and Their Promise for Medicine.* New York: John Henry Press, 2004.

Spangenburg, Ray, and Kit Moser. *Genetic Engineering.* New York: Benchmark Books, 2004.

Viegas, Jennifer. *Stem Cell Research.* New York: Rosen, 2003.

Internet Addresses

Stem Cell Information Home Page
    <http://stemcells.nih.gov/index>

Time.com—Stem Cell Science
    <http://www.time.com/time/2001/stemcells>

Today's Stem Cell Research
    <http://www.stemnews.com>

Index